Sikhism Today

D0813771

Continuum *Religion Today*

These useful guides aim to introduce religions through the lens of contemporary issues, illustrated throughout with examples and case studies taken from lived religion. The perfect companion for the student of religion, each guide interprets the teachings of the religion in question in a modern context and applies them to modern day scenarios.

Available now:
Christianity Today, George D. Chryssides
Hinduism Today, Stephen Jacobs
Islam Today, Ron Geaves
Judaism Today, Dan Cohn-Sherbok

Sikhism Today

Jagbir Jhutti-Johal

continuum

Continuum International Publishing Group

The Tower Building
11 York Road
London SE1 7NX

80 Maiden Lane
Suite 704
New York NY 10038

www.continuumbooks.com

British Library Cataloguing-in-Publication Data
A catalogue record for this book is available from the British Library.

ISBN: HB: 978-1-8470-6271-0
         PB: 978-1-8470-6272-7

Library of Congress Cataloguing-in-Publication Data
Jhutti-Johal, Jagbir.
  Sikhism today / Jagbir Jhutti-Johal.
     p. cm.
  ISBN 978-1-84706-272-7 — ISBN 978-1-84706-271-0 1. Sikhism. I. Title.
  BL2017.45.J48 2011
  294.6 — dc22

                              2010045169

Typeset by Newgen Imaging Systems Pvt Ltd, Chennai, India
Printed and bound in Great Britain

For
Karamveer and Amarveer

Contents

Preface

Sikhism has a rich and distinctive history, during which it has forged a unique identity while interacting with the other major religions of India – Hinduism and Islam – as well as impacting in a major way on the culture of the colonial power that was eighteenth- and nineteenth-century Britain.

To put into context, Sikhism was founded in the fifteenth century by Nanak, the first 'Guru' of Sikhism who, following a divine revelation, set out to preach the oneness of God and the importance of truthful living. He was able to bring together a number of schools of religious thought and philosophy, namely of *nirguna sampradaya*, the *sant* tradition. Today Sikhism is widely thought of as the most highly articulated expression of this tradition. Guru Nanak rejected the need to perform rituals such as idol worship, pilgrimages and fasting in the quest for spiritual liberation. Instead, he advocated meditation, *nam simran* and truthful living as the route to enlightenment (Banerjee 1983, McLeod 1997, Singh 1977).

Guru Nanak was succeeded by nine Gurus, and as the number of Sikhs grew, institutions and structures were put in place to consolidate this growth. The tenth and final Guru, Guru Gobind, established the *Khalsa* in 1699 CE, which cemented a militaristic dimension within Sikhism. This was partially in response to the threat posed to Sikhism's survival by the rulers of India, the Mughals. The *Khalsa* gave Sikhs an external identity which supported the internal identity as given by Guru Nanak. After the fall of the Mughals, Sikhs, under the rule of Ranjit Singh, established a large empire in Northern India, but this was only to be short lived (1799–1849) and was subsequently annexed by the British (McLeod 1997).

In the twentieth century the British exploited the military prowess of the Sikhs and many Sikhs were recruited to serve in the army and police, both in India and abroad. This relationship with the British, coupled with economic need, resulted in many Sikhs migrating to the United Kingdom after the 1950s. There are now more than 400,000 Sikhs in the United Kingdom and as a community they are well established.[1] Sikhs are now a fundamental part of pluralist British identity and are represented at all levels of British society. They have also been subject to a variety of media portrayals and interests, such as the Sikh warriors of Peter Dickinson's 1970s *The Changes* (a BBC trilogy); the Sikh family portrayed in *Bend It Like Beckham*; and the Bollywood film *Singh Is King*, which had a cover song involving the rap star Snoop Dogg. But Sikhism is more than either an Indian or UK-based phenomenon, there is a sizeable presence of Sikhs in other European nations such as France, Italy and Germany. Sikhs have also migrated in large numbers to other Western countries, such as the United States, Canada and Australia, to Singapore and Malaysia, and countries in Africa, such as Kenya.

While Sikhs appear to be a thriving global community which is influencing the social and political culture of the countries in which they reside, it is also evident that there is a readdressing among third- and fourth-generation Sikh migrants, but also by Sikhs in Punjab, India, of their own religious identity and values, and hence this is of great academic interest.

In recent years there has been a rapid rise in books on Sikhism, particularly in the West. This book will move away from a general historical introduction to Sikhism, which I believe has been adequately covered elsewhere. Instead, it will introduce the subject of Sikhism through the lens of contemporary issues confronting Sikhs. Issues will be discussed from a theological perspective, rather than just the cultural one which has defined the theological debate. However, some of the analysis will have to be supported by socio-cultural issues and values which also have been misinterpreted to have religious meanings/background.

For example, the rapid advances of medicine and biology present new challenges for the Sikh faith. There is general agreement on topics such as euthanasia and the making of a 'living will' or 'advance directive'. Life is seen as a gift from God and an opportunity to strive for enlightenment. Illness, suffering and pain are a result of one's actions (*karma*) in this or a previous life, and should be endured with moral courage and fortitude. The ultimate point of release from this life is the will of God (*hukam*) and should not be interfered with. Thus, assisted suicide and euthanasia are forbidden. However, on the subject of artificial prolonging of life, the argument is not so unequivocal. Some Sikhs may argue that in cases where further treatment is uncompassionate or medically ineffective, then the artificial prolonging of life should not be encouraged and the patient should be allowed to die naturally. In other instances the artificial prolonging of life may be encouraged and seen as necessary. Whatever the decision, the duty of family, friends and medical practitioners is to do everything to alleviate suffering while providing emotional and spiritual support during the last stages of life.

Other issues, such as genetic engineering and stem cell research, trigger lively debate among Sikhs and as yet no clear consensus has emerged on these issues. Most Sikhs will continue to make a personal choice on these matters.

Methodology

It is from this context, and the fact that there is a dearth of serious literature looking at how Sikhs deal with modern-day issues, that this book is written.

As a British-born member of the Sikh community, I located myself within my own religious community to carry out research on how the community and the religion operate when confronted by modern-day issues and how individuals deal with them using the Guru Granth Sahib as a guide. This book will describe the Gurus' philosophy and teachings, but it will be new and novel in that it will apply the basic tenets and teachings to current issues. When looking at current issues it will become clear that there is a plurality of interpretations of the teachings contained with the Guru Granth Sahib. Individuals reading the Guru Granth Sahib can arrive at different meanings and interpretations of the text, and it is because of this plurality that Sikhs will need to find a common language and come to a consensus on what things mean.

The primary source of reference for this study is the Guru Granth Sahib, the holy book of the Sikhs.[2] The Guru Granth Sahib is the Sikhs' perpetual guide and the epitome of the spiritual teachings of Sikhism. It is at the centre of all Sikh ceremonies. Secondary sources include the *Dasam Granth*, a book attributed to the tenth Guru, Guru Gobind Singh; *Janam Sakhis* (hagiographical life account of Guru Nanak); and other key references (e.g. Bhai Gurdas Ji's writings) are also consulted. I have chosen verses from the Guru Granth Sahib on such themes as liberation/salvation, morality and God and analyse them from a modern-day perspective. For example, there are many verses which discuss how liberation can only be achieved by living the life of a 'householder'. These verses will be used to discuss the disparity between what is written in the Guru Granth Sahib and what has actually been achieved in relation to the position of women and family. I will also use verses to interpret and discuss issues such as in vitro fertilization (IVF) and homosexuality.

To support the primary sources, I have undertaken some limited fieldwork to gather information on how individuals interpret the teachings contained in the sacred scriptures. I interviewed first-, second-, third- and fourth-generation Sikhs from various castes, social classes, age groups and localities in the United Kingdom and had informal discussions with *granthis* (priests). While all my first-generation informants, especially the *granthis*, were born and brought up in India, all my second-, third- and fourth-generation informants were born in Britain, although some had spent a short time in their parents' country of birth. My fieldwork is limited and I am aware that my respondents' comments may not be representative of all Sikhs, but nevertheless they are useful in highlighting the variety of views and opinions regarding modern-day issues that are present within the community.

My selection of respondents was not systematic. The interviews with elders were conducted in Punjabi, but some were conducted in English. Interviews with my second-, third- and fourth-generation respondents were mainly conducted in English, but some respondents did regularly lapse into Punjabi.

The responses to the interviews were intensely personal and revealing. All respondents discussed how they felt about issues such as homosexuality and abortion. However, it was the young Sikhs who discussed their own experiences and talked about their beliefs and interpretations with surprising frankness, unlike their parents.

In some places, where respondents' answers to my interviews are used, names are not provided due to confidentiality. I have endeavoured to keep the quotes in the spirit in which they were told. I am aware of the problems of de-contextualization, and the danger of using quotes to support any given argument or to make generalizations that this is a commonly-held belief for all Sikhs.

Thus, through the available primary and secondary literature, and through fieldwork, I will describe how the teachings of the Gurus are observed and how modern-day issues are being addressed through a reinterpretation of teachings contained within the Guru Granth Sahib.

Structure

Chapter 1 provides an overview of the Sikh religion, its history and basic theological tenets. The subsequent chapters attempt to interpret the teachings of Sikhism in a modern context and apply them to modern-day scenarios.

Chapter 2 broadly explores the interaction and growing conflict between religion and science, with particular reference to Sikhism. It then examines the tenets of Sikhism in relation to the ethics of genetic and stem cell research, cloning, IVF and animal testing. Very little research has been done on how science and the advances in biology and medicine, such as stem cell research and genetic engineering, present new challenges to Sikhs in terms of interpreting scriptures and teachings to form a consensus on these issues.

Chapter 3 looks at the concept of gender equality within Sikhism. At the time of Guru Nanak, society demeaned and degraded women through a variety of activities. Guru Nanak did not approve of this treatment of women, and in an attempt to raise their position within society he reiterated that his teachings on liberation, salvation and morality were equally relevant for men and women. The chapter then looks at the current status and role of women in Sikh society and presents actual case studies to highlight the continuing practice of gender inequality; for example, the case of baptized Sikh women not being allowed to perform certain *sewa* at the Harmandar Sahib (Golden Temple). Most importantly the attitudes and actions of the Gurus responding to gender inequality that existed in their time is discussed with reference to the current issue of female foeticide and gender preselection.

As with other religions, Sikhism faces issues of morality and ethics among its adherents. Issues include homosexuality, abortion, contraception and so forth. Chapter 4 examines these issues in relation to Sikh teachings from the Guru Granth Sahib and guidance provided by the Sikh religious authorities. This chapter was a challenge due to the lack of available research and unwillingness of some respondents to talk about issues such as abortion, euthanasia and homosexuality. However, this may have been due to their own limited understanding of these topics with reference to Sikh teachings. Despite the difficulties and limitations, the chapter highlights the issues involved and provides a basis for further research on such topics in the future.

Chapter 5 considers the question, 'Who Is a Sikh?' The chapter introduces the reader to the significance of baptism and the five articles of faith for Sikhs, and the historical struggles undertaken to maintain their Sikh religious identity. When discussing this, legal cases (turban and *kara* cases) are discussed with reference to their impact on the idea of who is a Sikh.The growing divide between baptized and non-baptized Sikhs and religious apathy, particularly among Sikh youth, are also considered when discussing the question of who is a Sikh.

The conclusion considers whether modern issues that are confronting the Sikhs, such as gender inequality, advances in science and technology, family life and homosexuality, can be addressed and understood through a critical engagement with the Guru Granth Sahib. It also considers whether the process of interpretation and reinterpretation has led to an abandonment, changing or impoverishment of the religious teachings from their original form.

The Gurus in the Sikh Religion

Name	Born	Period of Guruship	Relationship
Guru Nanak	1469	1539–	Follower of Nanak
Guru Angad	1504	1539–1552	Guru Angad's son-in-law's uncle[3]
Guru Amar Das	1479	1552–1574	Guru Amar Das' son-in-law
Guru Ram Das	1534	1574–1581	Guru Ram Das' son
Guru Arjan	1563	1581–1606	Guru Arjan's son
Guru Hargobind	1595	1606–1644	The younger son of Guru Hargobind's eldest son
Guru Har Rai	1630	1644–1661	Guru Har Rai's son
Guru Har Krishan	1656	1661–1664	Guru Hargobind's youngest son
Guru Tegh Bahadur	1621	1664–1675	Guru Tegh Bahadur's son
Guru Gobind Singh	1666	1675–1708	Sikh Holy Book (Eternal Guru)
Guru Granth Sahib		1708–eternity	

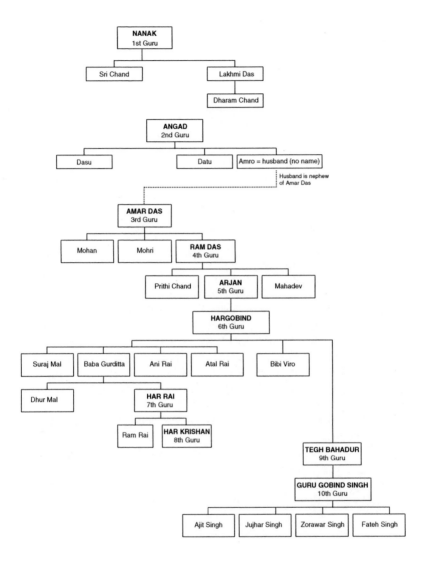

Genealogical Table of the Gurus

Acknowledgements

I am deeply grateful to many people for their support while I was writing this book.

I thank all my family. Most importantly, I thank my husband, Sukhvinder Johal, and my two sons, Karamveer and Amarveer, for their support and encouragement in my desire to pursue a quest for knowledge and understanding of Sikhism. They have been pillars of strength. Without their patience and support I would not have been able to complete this book.

I am deeply indebted to all those who shared with me their views. I am grateful to them for devoting their time to patiently answering my endless questions and discussing with me various issues, both sensitive and otherwise.

A substantial part of Chapter 1 was published in A. R. Gatrad et al. (eds), *Palliative Care for South Asians: Muslims, Hindus and Sikhs*, Quay Books (2005). It is produced with the permission of Quay Books, to whom I am extremely grateful.

Finally, I thank Kirsty Schaper at Continuum and Molly Morrison at Newgen for their patience, understanding and support.

Chapter 1

The Sikh Grand Narrative

Introduction

Sikhism is one of the world's youngest religions. Its founding Guru, or enlightener, Nanak, was born in 1469 CE in Punjab (which means quite literally 'a land of five rivers'), an area which resides across India and Pakistan. From a small movement of kindred spirits, Sikhism has now grown into a religion of about 20 million people (www.sikhs.org.uk). In their short and turbulent history, the Sikh people have been key players in many major Indian events of the past 500 years, including the fall of the Moghul Empire, the rise of the Sikh Empire in Punjab under Ranjit Singh, the rise and fall of the British Empire and the Indian independence struggle. Over the past century, Sikhs have migrated overseas in substantial numbers. As a result of this diaspora, Sikhs are to be found in several countries outside India, primarily in the United Kingdom, the United States, Canada, East Africa and Malaysia. Sikhism has its roots firmly embedded in Eastern philosophy. It shares many of its theological concepts, such as *samsara* (the cycle of birth and rebirth), *karma* (the law of action) and *moksha* (liberation or salvation), with faiths such as Hinduism and Buddhism, although its interpretations of these concepts may be different. In common with many Semitic faiths, it is an ardently monotheistic tradition which advocates the belief that God created the universe and everything that exists within it. God is thought to be beyond human comprehension and formless (*nirankar*). Sikhs can accept that the central figures of other faiths, such as Krishna, Moses, Jesus and Mohammed, were messengers of God with a divine mission. However, they do not accept the authority of any of the scriptures from other religions, looking instead for enlightenment and guidance from the Guru, which is manifested in the Guru Granth Sahib (GGS), the holy book of the Sikhs. Sikhs also do not believe that God takes a human form and hence reject the idea of, for example, the divinity of Jesus Christ or the gods or avatars of Hinduism. The word Sikh is derived from the Sanskrit word *Shishya*, which means a 'disciple' or 'learner'. This embodies the mindset of Sikhs, who are on a continual quest towards enlightenment.

A Short History

The history of Sikhism is one of enlightened souls, spiritual reinvigoration, beautiful poetic literature, martyrdom and struggle against persecution. Sikhs derive tremendous strength from their history. Guru Nanak was born during a relatively peaceful period in northern India following waves of invasions from Turks and Afghans as well as internal anarchy. Despite this original peace, the years of war and toil had left an indelible mark on its people. The period was one of great uncertainty, ignorance and moral disintegration. Society was fragmented not just by the rivalry of the two main religions, Hinduism and Islam, but also by the divisions within these religions. The caste system led to religious and racial segregation, the performing of perfunctory rituals in the name of God had permeated through society and superstitious practices were rife. For Guru Nanak, the world had entered into a dark age, in which most people had become disenfranchized from the path to salvation, and religion had lost its true purpose, the path of truth:

> The times are like drawn knives, kings like butchers,
> Righteousness has fled on wings,
> The dark night of falsehood prevails,
> The moon of truth is nowhere visible. (GGS, p. 145)

Nanak's life coincided with a period of religious renaissance in Europe – Martin Luther (1483–1546) and John Calvin (1509–64) being among his contemporaries (Singh 1999). He challenged current theologies and preached the message that the liberation of the soul was open to all, irrespective of race, sex, caste or religion. He may have drawn some inspiration from *Sufism*, a branch of Islamic mysticism and the *Bhakti*, or 'devotion to God' movement that had originated in southern India. However, he ultimately fashioned out his own philosophy elevating *truth* to the highest status and recognizing God as one. In practical terms Nanak convinced people that the Creator was immanent and accessible to everyone, encouraged charitable works and selfless service, and promoted the cause of women.

Before his death, Nanak appointed a successor, Angad, to continue his mission. In all there were ten human Gurus each accorded equal status among Sikhs. In fact, for many Sikhs the Gurus are seen as the spirit of Nanak assuming ten forms, and in the Guru Granth Sahib subsequent Gurus are referred to as Nanak I, Nanak II and so forth. Each Guru advanced the faith and added various facets to it. Angad collected Nanak's hymns into a book and added his own compositions. He also gave Sikhs a new script, *Gurmukhi* (from the mouth of the Guru). This gave the Sikhs a written language distinct from the written language of Hindus and Muslims and thus fostered a sense of them being a separate people (Singh 1977).

As the number of Sikhs began to grow, the third Guru, Guru Amar Das, began the institutionalization of the Sikh faith. He appointed territorial ministers, made the system of *langar*, or Guru's free kitchen, an integral part of religion. He also introduced various social reforms such as the prohibition of *sati*, the burning of widows on their husbands' funeral pyres, allowed remarriage of widows, advocated monogamy, denounced the veiling of women and appointed women preachers.

Ram Das, the fourth Guru, established a village, which was eventually to become the city of Amritsar, the spiritual and political capital of the Sikhs. The fifth Guru, Arjan, oversaw the construction of the holiest shrine in Sikhism, the Harmandar Sahib, known as the Golden Temple. Arjan was a prolific writer and composed more hymns than any of his predecessors. His most important achievement was the compilation of the *Adi Granth*. Guru Amar Das had compiled the *Mohan Pothi* which contained the hymns of Guru Nanak, Guru Angad, Guru Amar Das, Kabeer, Namdev, Jai Dev, Ravidas, Trilochan and Sain. Between 1601 and 1604 the fifth Guru, Guru Arjan, then selected, compiled, endorsed the selected writings and added hymns from Guru Ram Das, his own compositions and those of Sheik Farid, Beni, Ramanand, Dhanna, Bhikan, Sadhna, Pipa, Parmanand and Surdas to the text. The works of Hindu and Muslim saints were included because they echoed the views of the Gurus. Guru Arjan named this compilation the *Adi Granth* (the first Granth, which today is known as the *Kartarpur Bir*). It was handwritten by Bhai Gurdas in a specific arrangement of thirty-one ragas, an order of authors and an order of poetic forms as prescribed by Guru Arjan Dev. The *Adi Granth* was installed at Harmandar Sahib, Amritsar, India, on 1 September 1604. It became the embodiment of Sikh thought, helping to catapult Sikh teachings to the masses. Arjan wrote of the Guru Granth Sahib:

> In this vessel, three things lie:
> truth, contentment, contemplation.
> They contain the ambrosial Name,
> By which we are all sustained.
> They who eat, they who savour, they are liberated.
> This thing must not be abandoned;
> Ever and ever, keep it in your heart. (GGS, p. 1,429)

The growing influence of Arjan brought him into conflict with the rulers of Punjab. Indeed his presence was a threat to their power. The Mughal Emperor Jehangir had Arjan arrested and, while in custody, he was put to death. Arjan is seen by Sikhs as their first martyr and his death marked a turning point for the Sikh community. They now felt a real and physical threat to their principles and way of life. The sixth Guru, Hargobind, in reaction to this, added a militaristic dimension to the Sikh faith. He introduced the concept of *miri/piri*: the individuals should have spiritual authority (*piri*) while assume a temporal role (*miri*). The period of guruship among the seventh and eight Gurus was generally one of peace and the continual spread of Sikh teachings. This peace was to be shattered during the tenure of the ninth Guru, Guru Tegh Bahadur. He died defending the rights of others to practice their own faith. Like the fifth Guru, Guru Tegh Bahadur was executed by the authorities. Guru Tegh Bahadur composed many hymns, which were later added to the Guru Granth Sahib by the tenth Guru.

The tenth Guru, Guru Gobind Singh, was instrumental in creating the *Khalsa* (the fraternity of the 'pure') which instructed Sikhs to take *pahul* (baptism) to create a community devoted to a life of prayer and service, while also always being prepared to fight injustice and defend the weak. He also introduced the outward symbols of Sikh identity worn by 'baptized' Sikhs, known as the Five Ks, the *kara* (steel bangle), *kirpan* (a small curved sword), *kesh* (uncut hair), *kangha* (comb) and *kachera* (cotton shorts/underwear). Further, to emphasize the equality of man and rejection of the caste system all men who joined the *Khalsa* were to add the name Singh or 'lion' to their forename and all women were to add Kaur or 'princess'. However, today virtually all

Sikhs whether baptized or not, will use Singh or Kaur as a middle name.

Guru Gobind Singh, also re-scribed the entire *Adi Granth* after reciting it through divine revelation. Within the new edition he included the hymns of the ninth Guru, Guru Tegh Bahadur. This was known as the *Damdama Bir*. On the eve of his death, Guru Gobind Singh decreed that no living Guru would follow him and that spiritual authority now rested with the *Guru Granth Sahib*, which would be the Sikhs' Eternal Guru (Banerjee 1983, McLeod 1997).

With each Guru there was most definitely a shift in emphasis of the Sikh movement. This was in part a natural evolution of a religious movement and in part a response to the changing political and environmental circumstances. However, it is quite clear from the Guru Granth Sahib that the core spiritual or religious ideology did not change.

The Guru Granth Sahib

The Guru Granth Sahib is the epitome of the spiritual teachings of Sikhism. It is the Sikhs' perpetual guide and contains the main doctrine of the Sikhs concerning God, God's nature and attributes and the means by which salvation may be attained (Field 1914). Sikhs view it as the repository of God's word transmitted through His messengers, the Gurus. As Nanak stated,

I speak, O God, only when you inspire me to speak. (GGS, p. 566)

Guru Granth Sahib is not written as a document recording history. The paucity of references within the Guru Granth Sahib describing contemporary historical events is an indication that the Gurus wished it to transcend these superficial issues and focus on the timeless and eternal creator. Indeed many would argue that the Guru Granth Sahib is simply an attempt to explain the first line in it, *Ik Onkar*, there is but one God.

The Guru Granth Sahib is the centre of focus at all Sikh ceremonies, including birth, marriage and death. It is held in such high veneration that it is wrapped in a fine cloth and Sikhs will prostrate themselves before it when entering its presence. Its hymns are usually expressed musically. The Guru Granth Sahib is testament to a unique feature of Sikhism, that the word of the Guru (or God), *Gurbani*, is the key to

---

A description of the Guru Granth Sahib given by Pearl S. Buck, winner of the Nobel Prize for Literature, 1938:

Shri Guru Granth Sahib is a source book, an expression of man's loneliness, his aspiration, his longings, his cry to God and his hunger for communication with that being. I have studied the scriptures of other great religions, but I do not find elsewhere the same power of appeal to the heart and mind as I feel here in these volumes. They are compact in spite of their length, and are a revelation of the vast reach of the human heart varying from the most noble concept of God to the recognition and indeed the insistence upon the practical needs of the human body. There is something strangely modern about these scriptures and this puzzled me until I learnt that they are in fact comparatively modern, compiled as late as the sixteenth century, when explorers were beginning to discover the globe upon which we all live as a single entity divided only by arbitrary lines of our own making. Perhaps this sense of unity is a source of power I find in these volumes. They speak to persons of any religion or of none. They speak for the human heart and the searching mind (Buck 1987).

---

salvation and not the Guru himself. The Guru is the instrument that God uses to spread His Word. Therefore handling this book and indeed all other religious books should be with utmost humility and respect.

Who Is a Sikh?

Sikhs can essentially be divided into two main groups: the baptized and the unbaptized. The *pahul* or baptism ceremony (*Amrit Sanskar*) is undertaken when an individual fully comprehends the implications of such an act.[1] Hence, it is rare for a prepubescent child to be baptized. There is no upper age limit to baptism and it is encouraged for both men and women. The ceremony takes place in the presence of the Guru Granth Sahib. The principles of the faith and other key instructions on how a baptized Sikh must live are imparted to the initiate. For example, these include devotion to God, service to mankind, struggle against injustice and defence of the weak. On acceptance of these instructions, *amrit* (nectar of immortality) is prepared by pouring water and sugar pellets into a steel bowl and stirring the mixture with a double-edged dagger while selected verses from the Guru Granth Sahib and *Dasam Granth* (collected works attributed to the tenth Guru) are read out aloud. The initiate drinks five handfuls of *amrit* and five handfuls are sprinkled over his or her hair and eyes. Further prayers are then offered followed by a random reading of a verse from the Guru Granth Sahib. If a person does not have a Sikh name, he or she takes a new name at this time. The candidate is now formally admitted to the *Khalsa* Community (Gatrad et al. 2005).

Baptized Sikhs (*amrit-dhari* or *Khalsa* Sikhs) constitute an 'orthodoxy' within Sikhism. Unbaptized Sikhs (who form the majority in the United Kingdom) are either *kesh-dhari* Sikhs (keep their hair unshorn and wear the outward symbols of the Sikh faith, i.e. the turban), or *mona* Sikhs (retain an affiliation to the *Khalsa* but remove the outward symbols of the faith) (Gatrad et al. 2005). All Sikhs will believe in one eternal God, the ten Gurus and accept the Guru Granth Sahib as their eternal Guru.

The Ultimate Reality

The central statement of the Sikh faith about God is given in the opening lines of the Guru Granth Sahib. Composed by the first Guru, Nanak, they provide a succinct summary of the very essence of Sikh beliefs about God:

> There is One Supreme Being
> Eternal Truth by Name
> Immanent in all beings
> Sustainer of all things
> Creator of all things
> Without fear
> Devoid of enmity
> Timeless in image
> Beyond birth and death
> Self-existent
> Made known by the grace of the Guru. (GGS, p. 1)

The unity and oneness of God is a theme continually repeated throughout the Guru Granth Sahib. God is also described as formless, without gender and, in common with many religions, beyond human comprehension. God is the creator and the cause of creation. The essence of God is known as *nam* and this pervades all creation. Sikhs believe that every soul is a divine spark of the eternal flame of the creator and the ultimate aim is for each spark to obtain union with its divine source.

The Human Condition and Spiritual Liberation

Sikhs believe in reincarnation and *karma*, in which the soul undergoes various births and rebirths, in both human and non-human forms, dependent on past actions. Birth can take the form of any one of 8.4 million life forms, half of which exist on land and the other half in water. The human form is seen as the only opportunity to achieve liberation (*Moksha*) from the cycle of birth, death and rebirth and union with God (*Sahaj*). Human beings are thought to be blessed because they have reason, wisdom and the potential for being aware of God. Guru Nanak preached the message that this liberation or salvation was open to all, irrespective of caste, creed or sex. However, the goal of liberation is not an easy one to achieve and ultimately depends upon God's grace.

The key obstacle to achieving liberation is *haumai*. This is a very difficult word to translate into English, but can be interpreted as some one who is an egoistic self-centred being. All men and women are born with *haumai*, which is God-created, and acts like a veil obfuscating the presence and vision of the divine that pervades all around and within each person. *Haumai* leads the mind and soul into delusion and worldly attachment. According to the Gurus, *haumai* is the great disease of humanity (Singh 1994). The goal of a Sikh is to overcome this *haumai*.

The Guru Granth Sahib elucidates how liberation can be achieved and calls for a self-centred approach to be replaced by a God-centred approach in life. The aim is to achieve a new state of consciousness and realize God within. The most important concept is that of *nam simran* or 'meditation of the True Name'. Some Sikhs will use the technique of constantly repeating God's Name but *nam simran* goes well beyond this. The mind must be wholly tuned to the essence of God so that the person becomes totally absorbed in Him. Now every thought and action has to be imbibed with God. Ultimately this is done without any mental effort or any conscious awareness and the result is a person who dedicates his/her life to God and the service of others. *Nam simran* is not something to be done alone or away from society and certainly does not advocate withdrawal from daily life. It should be accompanied by participation in the life of *sangat*, the fellowship of believers (Cole and Sambhi 1978), and as an active member of the community.

Guru Nanak describes five realms or levels of spiritual experience as one traverses the path to union with God. The final level, the realm of truth, leads to the realization of the Truth and complete harmony with God. In contrast to many religious traditions one does not have to wait for death to achieve this state of being. Liberation is available in this present life. Death only marks the final release.

The discipline of *nam simran* and the final goal of union with God is certainly not an easy one. Many Sikhs accept that they will not reach the realm of truth. However, for them the goal is certainly one worth striving for and they recognize that sincere efforts can make it achievable.

Sikhism rejects asceticism, renunciation of worldly life, celibacy or the separation from one's family or home to achieve union with God. Married life, *grihasta*, is celebrated and encouraged.

Sikh Practices

In a multicultural society where people of different faiths may look after a very ill Sikh patient and perhaps continue to interact with the family after death, the section hereunder will, we hope, be of practical help. All religious movements, if they are to last, ultimately develop a set of rules and practices to give the message of their founders permanency and also to bond the disciples of that movement closer together. Sikhism is no different in this regard. Most of these practices emanate from the time of the Gurus but have been formalized in the last two centuries. They are a reinforcement of the teachings of the Gurus.

The central pillar of Sikhism is *nam-simran* – a quest to connect with the Creator overriding all else. This should be coupled with a life dedicated to truth and service of others. Sikhism rejects the idea that fasting, bathing at religious sites, religious penances or pilgrimages have any spiritual merit:

> If salvation can be achieved by bathing in water, then a frog is better off. He remains in water all the time. (GGS, p. 484)

The daily routine of a Sikh dates back to a practice introduced by Guru Nanak. While every Sikh should attempt to keep God in his thoughts constantly throughout the day, there are three set prayers to aid meditation. First, he will rise at dawn and after taking a bath, will meditate by reciting a selection of hymns composed by Guru Nanak and Guru Gobind Singh. Next, at sunset, he/she will recite the *Rahiras* (the Holy Path) and finally, before going to bed, will repeat a prayer called *Sohilla*. While there are no ritual ablutions before prayer, bathing is seen as essential for personal hygiene and in helping reinvigorate the mind and body for meditation. The daily prayers can be performed individually, collectively as a family or at the gurdwara (Sikh place of worship).

The gurdwara,[2] meaning 'doorway to the Guru', is the centre for all Sikh worship and it is where the Guru Granth Sahib is installed. For Sikhs, the gurdwara represents a place for meditation and contemplation where one can be infused and energized by listening to the recitation of the Guru Granth Sahib. Inside the gurdwara, worshippers will approach the Guru Granth Sahib and genuflect or prostrate themselves fully before it, before sitting down themselves. This should not be confused with idol worship – this act is performed to accept the authority of the Guru Granth Sahib and its teachings. The general convention is to sit on the floor, but for the infirm or disabled, chairs or wheelchairs are permitted. Men and women usually sit on separate sides of the Guru Granth Sahib, which is more in line with Indian culture than with any aspect of belief. There is no fixed day for worship, but in the West, congregations usually gather in large numbers on Sunday reflecting the cultural context in which Sikhs live. Music and the singing of hymns are seen as integral to meditation and worship. Music is seen as a way of lifting hearts and minds and helping to ease one's attention towards God.

Sikhism has no priesthood or ordained ministers. Any baptized lay member of the congregation may lead the worship, male or female. In practice, many gurdwaras, especially in the West, employ a *granthi* (priest), usually male, whose responsibilities include reading the scriptures, performing ceremonies and the upkeep of the gurdwara. However, his role should not be confused with that of a priest. He does not have any special religious authority above that of an ordinary lay member but will invariably be well versed in the scriptures.

In keeping with the principle of equality, the gurdwara is open to all people of any religion (or of none), nationality, caste, gender, etc. This openness is extended to the *langar*, or 'Guru's free kitchen' in which vegetarian food is prepared and served to the congregation. All partakers will sit together on the floor and eat – this is another expression of equality. The *langar* is an integral part of worship.

It is worth mentioning at this point, that while the founders of Sikhism set out to establish a society based on equality and free of caste hierarchies, in practice Sikhs have absorbed some aspects of Hindu caste practices. Sikh villages in India are still divided in much the same way as Hindu villages (Bhachu 1985), with different castes sitting on different rungs of the social ladder. These ideas also persist in the minds of Sikhs outside India including the United Kingdom. Traditionally, the *jats* (agriculturists) have resided at the top of this caste hierarchy and form the majority of the Sikh population in India and the United Kingdom. They are followed by castes such as *ramgarhias* (artisans/craftsmen), many of whom migrated from East Africa. Below these two major groups are the so-called *outcaste* groups such as *bhatras* (peddlers) and *chamars* (leather workers) (Bhachu 1985). To an outsider it is very difficult to distinguish between these different groups. However, different caste groups can be recognized by family or clan name. Another pointer is the different styles of turbans worn by men in different caste groups as well as subtle differences in styles of dress. Although different caste groups will mix freely, work, eat and worship together, when it comes to marriage, they will not. Marriages are caste endogamous and marriage between members of different castes is taboo. There are some tentative signs that this may be changing as class (education, profession, wealth), rather than caste becomes more important among young Sikh professionals.

Sikhism does not prescribe any days as being specifically auspicious or holy. Each day is seen as another opportunity to praise the creator and develop a relationship with Him. However, Sikhs are particularly drawn together on their major festivals. These include the birthdays of the Gurus (*Gurpurbs*) and *Baisakhi* (creation of the *Khalsa*). These festivals are seen as an opportunity to reflect on the Gurus teachings, Sikh history and sacrifice.

Conclusion

Sikhism has come a long way in a short span of time. From the message that Guru Nanak preached over five hundred years ago, it has now sprung into a cohesive and powerful religion, which still retains diversity within it. For most Sikhs their religion is a journey in search of truth, representing an opportunity to connect with the creator and achieve liberation. It also signifies a life of high moral conduct, active service and righteous living, and these values will be explored in subsequent chapters with reference to science, gender and identity.

Chapter 2

Sikhism and Science

Introduction

The rapid progress of science and technology has posed many questions and challenges for religious people, both from the perspective of questioning their faith-based beliefs and in terms of raising ethical and moral questions concerning the use of new technology. For the most part, Sikhs have not engaged in the science/religion debate. As a relatively young religion – circa fifteenth century – the energy of the Sikhs has been concentrated on defending their faith from persecution, which they faced in the seventeenth and eighteenth centuries, and on setting up institutions and structures to give Sikhism a unique identity and protect it from being absorbed by other larger faiths such as Hinduism. The *Rehat Maryada*, the code of conduct for the Sikhs, makes no mention of how Sikhs should view matters such as evolution or genetic engineering. It is only now, as Sikhs have moved from being, on the whole, a semi-literate community in Punjab to a well-educated workforce, particularly in the diaspora, that these issues have begun to be addressed.

The first section of this chapter will look broadly at the interaction of Sikhism and science, particularly in reference to fundamental questions of the origin of the universe and humanity. Darwin's theory of evolution has engendered intriguing philosophical questions about the nature of humanity and our position in relation to the rest of the animal world, which appears to conflict with the traditional, religious idea that places humanity at the pinnacle of creation. This section will examine Sikh views on creation and the challenges Sikh teachings may face in an increasingly scientific, evidence-based world.

Advances in stem cell research offer potentially new cures and therapies for previously incurable diseases. However, the destruction of the embryo in the process of harvesting stem cells raises key ethical questions about the moral status of the embryo and the nature of humanity itself. The second section of this chapter addresses some of the key ethical concerns regarding genetic engineering, stem cell research and cloning and will tackle these concerns from a distinctly Sikh perspective. It will also address issues around assisted reproductive technologies and the ethical dilemmas that Sikhs may have in using such technologies.

Sikhism and the Origin of Man

The theory of evolution, an expanded version of the work of Charles Darwin (1985), is accepted by virtually all scientists, and holds the notion that all life on earth is related and has descended from a common ancestor or common gene pool. Humans are not considered to be somehow separate from other organisms on earth. As stated by Baptiste et al. (2005), humans, along with all other species present today, are simply a stage in the process of evolution, with their diversity the product of a long series of speciation and extinction events.

All major world religions believe that humanity sits at the apex of creation, as an intended and special species, sentient and self-aware. For Western, monotheistic religions, humans are the only 'creatures' on earth that are able to achieve salvation and admittance to heaven upon death. For Sikhs, who believe in reincarnation as many Eastern religious practitioners do, humans are seen as the ultimate point in creation, and while the soul can reside in any life form on earth, it must achieve human status to stand any chance of liberation and ultimate union with God. In contrast to the theological viewpoint, the corollary of the theory of evolution is that humanity only resides on one tiny branch of the evolutionary tree, having gone through as many evolutionary steps as say a bacterium. Undoubtedly, humans are among the most complex of animals but only with regard to the nervous system. This raises key questions about the nature of humanity.

The question of evolution and religion has not raised any major concerns in the past for Sikh masses. Religion and science have been kept distinctly separate and have not warranted a full debate, probably due to the fact that, up until now, scientific thought and practices have not developed and permeated through Sikh society to the same extent as they have in the West. The theory of evolution has posed no practical or moral issues for Sikhism and thus has been largely ignored. Most

Sikhs generally believe that all science will end in the ultimate truth of God. However, with increasing globalization and the spread of the Sikh diaspora, Sikhism will increasingly come under the same scrutiny from the evidence-based methodologies of science as other religious philosophies have.

Like all religious texts, the Guru Granth Sahib, is not set out as a scientific document based on physical (or measurable) evidence about the world. Instead it deals in metaphysics and philosophical propositions. Its aim is to appeal to the human heart and consciousness, to elevate the human condition by emphasizing the importance of God centricity and faith. For Sikhs, the boundary between this faith-based world view and a scientific or evidence-based world view has traditionally been a distinct one and conflict between these two views has generally not occurred. However, as this dividing line begins to blur, Sikhism faces the same challenge as other religions in convincing an increasingly scientifically literate population of the validity and relevance of its core messages about God and the relationship between man, nature and God.

A number of authors and contributors to Internet-based discussions[1] have attempted to correlate verses in the Guru Granth Sahib to current scientific theory about the origin of the universe, evolution and even quantum mechanics. Although this is a highly unscientific methodology, it is useful to outline the verses in the Guru Granth Sahib in order to provide a framework of Sikh belief on such matters, and to examine how they are now being interpreted within a scientific context.

The Origin of the Universe

The kernel of Sikh teachings is that God is the creator who pervades all creation. Nothing exists without Him and it was through His will, referred to as *Hukam*, that the Universe was created. As stated in the Guru Granth Sahib:

> He created the creation, and watches over it; the Hukam of His Command is over all. (GGS, p. 1,035)

In another verse, Guru Nanak describes the process of creation of the universe.

You created the vast expanse of the Universe with One Word!
Hundreds of thousands of rivers began to flow. (GGS, p. 3)

For a number of Sikhs, the above verses sit comfortably with the idea
of the Big Bang theory of creation and development of the Universe.
The Big Bang theory is a cosmological model describing the development of the universe from its early beginnings to its continual expan-
sion and is the most widely accepted theory by scientists, backed by a
comprehensive set of scientific evidence and observations (Hawkins
1995). The theory asserts that the universe has a finite beginning and
was created from a single point in which all matter and energy were
concentrated around 14 billion years ago. Sikhs could easily equate
this single event of creation with the 'One Word' in the quote above.
Further, the line 'Hundreds of thousands of rivers began to flow' could
be taken as a metaphor for a growing and expanding cosmos.

However, the key issue that separates science and Sikhism is the
original cause of the big bang itself. For scientists, what existed prior
to this event is completely unknown and is a matter of pure conjecture
at present. In fact, from a scientific viewpoint, the question itself may
be invalid because the big bang not only engendered matter and energy
but also time itself and so without time existing before the big bang it
is impossible to use the phrase 'before the big bang' in any meaningful
way (Simon Singh 2004). Traditionally, this is where theology and religion has stepped in, ascribing a supernatural trigger to the creation of
the universe.

The Guru Granth Sahib speaks of a time before the universe was
created, or in other words, a time before the 'big-bang':

For endless eons, there was only utter darkness.
There was no earth or sky; there was only the infinite Command
of His *Hukam*.
There was no day or night, no moon or sun; God sat in primal,
profound *Samaadhi*.
There were no sources of creation or powers of speech, no air or
water.
There was no creation or destruction, no coming or going.
There were no continents, nether regions, seven seas, rivers or
flowing water.
There were no heavenly realms, earth or nether regions of the
underworld.
There was no heaven or hell, no death or time.

There was no hell or heaven, no birth or death, no coming or
going in reincarnation.
There was no Brahma, Vishnu or Shiva.
No one was seen, except the One Lord. (GGS, p. 1,035)

The verse, by Guru Nanak, describes the universe as a void of nothing-
ness in which only God resides in a state of *Samaadhi* (contemplation
or meditation), a place where there is not even the concept of time. The
verse is highly symbolic, it reiterates the infinite magnitude and power
of God as well as His eternal nature. God is the creator and the source,
without whom nothing would exist.

Evolution and the Origin of Life

The theory of origin and creation of man has been postulated by most
of the major world religions and they all have one thing in common:
the central role played by a divine being in man's creation. Most religions also describe the state of being a human as the highest form of
God's creation holding a privileged place among the rest of creation.

The scientific theory of evolution challenges religious scripture as it
negates the requirement of an interventionist creator nor does it
ascribe to the 'belief' that human beings are the highest and the most
complex form of life that have reached the highest branch of the evolutionary tree.

Sikhism subscribes to the theory that God is the progenitor of all life
and pervades all creation. Within its current framework it can certainly accept that man could have evolved from 'lower' life forms. The
idea of reincarnation presupposes that all life forms are interrelated
and that man is the culmination of a progression through all of them.
Sikhism can also absorb the biological concept of 'Natural Selection'
in which favourable heritable traits become more common in successive
generations of a population of reproducing organisms, and unfavour-
able heritable traits become less common, due to differential reproduction of genotypes (Futuyma 2005). However, there are some very
important caveats to be made here. Sikhism does not prescribe to the
theory that gene mutations, the first step of the evolutionary process,
are random events nor that chance plays a huge part in evolution. For
Sikhs, evolution is the result of a divine law, a law that controls its
processes and outcomes.

He created the creation, and watches over it.
The *Hukam* of His Command is over all. (GGS, p. 1,036)

Emphasis is placed on an interventionist designer and creator of the world. And chance plays no part, the creation of human beings is part of the divine plan: for Sikhs it does not follow that if a huge asteroid hadn't struck the Earth 60 million years ago, dinosaurs might still rule the Earth! Another conflict with evolutionary theory is that, for Sikhs, humans occupy a privileged position in the tree of life and represent the final stage of creation before God realization. In Sikhism, the ultimate goal of evolution was to produce humanity. Current evolutionary theory does not prescribe to this view. There is no ultimate goal in evolutionary theory (Dawkins 1997):

After wandering and wandering for so long, you have come
In this Dark Age of Kali Yuga, you have obtained this human
body, so very difficult to obtain.
This opportunity shall not come into your hands again.
So chant the *Nam*, the Name of the Lord, and the noose of Death
shall be cut away. (GGS, p. 258)

For the majority of Sikhs today, the questions that modern science might raise in connection with their religious outlook on life are not a key concern. This may be due to the fact that focus of science on challenging religious orthodoxies and theories have been centred on the texts of the Semitic faiths and perhaps because the Sikh community itself has not produced scientists who wish to challenge or question its religious philosophies. There may be another reason however. The Guru Granth Sahib is a document that appeals to the emotions of humanity, to address the longings that human beings have to explain the mysteries of life from a philosophical perspective and to provide a guide on leading a 'good' life. The Guru Granth Sahib is replete with symbolic language, metaphors and poetry that appeal directly to the heart. It is not written as a scientific document, the Gurus were mystics who were more fascinated with the wonders of creation than its origins. The majority of Sikhs today see the discipline of science as distinct from religion, which helps to aid their understanding of the world and have no concerns about its findings. However, Sikhs also see the religious philosophy of the Guru Granth Sahib, as providing an 'ultimate truth' that transcends scientific rationale. For Sikhs, rightly or wrongly, there is no contradiction between the two.

Religious philosophies and viewpoints are increasingly coming under the spotlight of the scientific microscope. How Sikhism adapts and responds to these challenges is a subject for future research.

Biomedical Technology

With the widespread use of artificial reproductive technologies such as in vitro fertilization and worldwide research in embryonic stem cells and human cloning, ethical concerns about these technologies, particularly with regards to the creation, manipulation and destruction of the embryo have come to the fore in recent years. From a practical viewpoint these topics are more pertinent for Sikhs today than the question of the origin of humanity as discussed above, simply because they raise direct moral and ethical questions about the conduct of humanity in its quest for scientific advancement and impinge directly on dilemmas that may be faced by the population at some point. At present, there are no explicit injunctions within Sikhism regarding such matters.

The following sections will attempt to address some of the moral and ethical questions around such technologies from a Sikh perspective.

Human Embryonic Stem Cell Research and Cloning

The discovery, isolation and culturing of human embryonic stem cells has been described as one of the most significant breakthroughs of the century in biomedicine (Okarma 2001) and offers much hope for alleviating the human suffering brought on by the ravages of disease and injury. It is hoped that one day stem cell research will alleviate the need for organ and tissue donation.

Stem cells are undifferentiated embryo-like cells that can divide to produce either cells like themselves (self-renewal), or cells of one or several specific differentiated and specialized types. This is particularly true of stem cells found in the embryo at around 5–7 days after fertilization where cells constituting the embryo start to be differentiated into inner and outer cells and are capable of differentiation into virtually all other body cell types (Corrigan et al. 2006). There are a number of potential other sources for stem cells in the adult body such as neural tissue, blood and skin, but as yet there is little evidence to suggest that these have the same development potential as embryonic cells. The harvesting of stem cells from human embryos, however, involves the destruction of the embryo itself at around five to seven days after fertilization and therefore this raises fundamental questions about the ethical acceptability of the process and indeed about the value of life itself (Corrigan et al. 2006).

In connection with embryonic stem cell research, salient ethical issues about artificial human cloning arise. Human cloning is a type of asexual reproduction that results in the production of an organism (human, human cell) that is a near (greater than 99.9 per cent) genetic copy of another organism (UNESCO 2005). Human cloning occurs in nature, human clones in the form of identical twins are commonplace, with their cloning occurring during the natural process of reproduction. However, it is not these natural processes that people generally refer to when speaking about cloning. They are referring to processes of manipulating nature to produce identical organisms, that is, artificial human cloning. There are two commonly discussed types of human cloning: therapeutic cloning and reproductive cloning (UNESCO 2005). Therapeutic cloning is the production of human embryos for use in research. The goal of this process is not to create cloned human beings, but rather to harvest stem cells that can be used to study human development and to treat disease. The embryo is unavoidably destroyed during this process. Reproductive cloning would involve making cloned humans. The clonal embryo is implanted in a woman's womb with the intention of creating a fully formed baby. Such reproductive cloning has not been performed and is illegal in many countries.

We will mainly consider the ethics of therapeutic cloning in this chapter as it is implicitly linked with embryo stem cell research and the destruction of the embryo.

Assisted Reproductive Technologies

Assisted reproductive technology (ART) encompasses a wide range of techniques designed primarily to help infertile couples conceive. It generally involves removing eggs from a woman's body, mixing them with sperm in the laboratory, and putting the embryos back into a woman's body, although the definition of ART could also be expanded to cover treatments in which only sperm are handled (i.e., intrauterine or artificial insemination). These technologies raise their own ethical issues, some related to the treatment of the embryo and others related to the question of parenting and the integrity of the family. We shall look at two technologies: artificial insemination (AI) and in vitro fertilization (IVF) which give rise to many of the ethical questions related to ART.

Artificial Insemination

Artificial insemination is a treatment for infertility that involves directly inserting sperm through a catheter or needle into a woman's womb   (www.nhs.uk/conditions/artificial-insemination/Pages/Intro-duction.aspx). When the man has a low sperm count or if he cannot produce sperm during sexual intercourse, the artificial insemination is done with the sperm of the husband or partner. However, in some circumstances, the man may not be able to produce any healthy sperm. If this is the case, frozen sperm, obtained from a donor, can be used. This donor may be a friend or relative or, as in most cases, sperm is taken from an 'anonymous' donor (www.nhs.uk/conditions/artificial insemination/Pages/Introduction.aspx). In the United Kingdom, the conditions of total anonymity no longer hold however, as any person who is born from donated sperm after 1 April 2005 is entitled to apply to the Human Fertilisation and Embryology Authority (HFEA) to obtain information about the identity of the donor, once he or she has reached eighteen years of age.

In Vitro Fertilization

In vitro fertilization is a process by which egg cells are fertilized by sperm outside the womb and the resulting embryo is transferred to the womb to grow and develop. The woman takes fertility drugs to stimu-late the production of as many healthy eggs as possible. These eggs are then inseminated with the male sperm resulting in a number of created embryos. One or two of these embryos are implanted in the woman's womb. Any remaining embryos suitable for freezing may be stored for future use. The sperm and/or eggs used may be the couple's own or donated.

Ethical Issues of Biomedical Technology

There is no Sikh teaching that directly addresses the morality of stem cell research or assisted reproductive technologies, but we may look at the central teachings of Sikhism to inform us how Sikhs may view this type of research. It would be natural for Sikhs to refer to the Guru Granth Sahib for support and guidance on all ethical matters. However, the Guru Granth Sahib is not written as a set of rules and regulations but attempts to explain the human experience in relation to God and the importance of the human form in the path to enlightenment.

The *Rehat Maryada*, or Sikh code of conduct, which has evolved from the period immediately following the death of the final Guru, Gobind Singh, and approved in 1950, is a document that consolidates many other *Rehats* written throughout Sikh history, and sets down what it means to be a Sikh and how Sikhs should lead their lives. It makes no reference to ethical questions around the issues of new technology and biological advances.

To capture the Sikh viewpoint on issues such as stem cell research one must attempt to interpret and extrapolate Sikh teachings, as encapsulated in the Guru Granth Sahib, and also to examine current Sikh thought and practices with reference to the unborn child, specifically at the embryo stage. There appear to be two key issues around the ethics of the biomedical technology being discussed here. First, there is the question of the moral status of the embryo as stem cell research, cloning and IVF involve the destruction and manipulation of the embryo outside the womb. Second, there is the question of kinship, and parenthood of embryos and children formed from the genetic material of third party donors, and this is inextricably linked to the concept of marriage and family in Sikhism.

When Does a Human Being Begin to Exist?

Many of the ethical issues around stem cell research and cloning overlap with those connected to IVF and raise questions about the moral status of the embryo and its rights. In stem cell research and therapeutic cloning the harvesting of stem cells from human embryos involves the destruction of the embryo at around five to seven days after fertilization. In IVF embryos that are not transferred to a woman's uterus may ultimately be used for research purposes or destroyed. Hence we may apply the same reasoning here for stem cell research and therapeutic cloning as we do for IVF when discussing the moral status of the embryo.

A premise of the argument against the destruction or manipulation of embryos is that human embryos are human beings and thus the issue of when a human being begins to exist is at the heart of the debate of whether it is justified to artificially create and terminate embryos for research. At one end of the spectrum is the belief that life begins at conception and is created by God, therefore an embryo should be accorded the full rights of a human being. Other believers of religion, such as in Islam and Judaism, assert that an embryo acquires 'person' status after a certain period of development. Science would argue that the embryo at such an early stage in its development is simply a collection of cells, non-sentient with no consciousness, which even in natural procreation has a greater probability of being destroyed than developing into a baby.

For Sikhs a human being is defined at the point in which the soul enters the body. It is the soul that is responsible for the mind and intellect, and the body acts as a medium through which the soul experiences the trials and tribulations of human existence. Death can destroy the body but not the soul. Therefore the key question that arises here is, according to Sikhism, when does the soul enter the body? Although there is some debate within the Sikh community regarding this question, the overriding consensus of Sikhs asserts that the life of a human being begins at the moment of conception:

> In the first watch of the night, O my merchant friend, you were cast into the womb, by the Lord's Command.
> Upside-down, within the womb, you performed penance, O my merchant friend, and you prayed to your Lord and Master.
> You uttered prayers to your Lord and Master, while upside-down, and you meditated on Him with deep love and affection.
> You came into this Dark Age of Kali Yuga naked, and you shall depart again naked.
> As God's Pen has written on your forehead, so it shall be with your soul. Says Nanak, in the first watch of the night, by the Hukam of the Lord's Command, you enter into the womb. (GGS, p. 74)

The Guru Granth Sahib appears to use the term body and soul interchangeably implying that in its 'earthly' existence the soul is intertwined with the body. The quote above states that the soul is cast in to the womb in the 'first watch of night', implying immediacy to the process. The quote below also lends weight to the fact that the created being is present in the womb for the full term of the pregnancy:

The Lord created the body from sperm, and protected it in the fire pit.[2] For ten months[3] He preserved you in your mother's womb, and then, after you were born, you became attached to *Maya*. (GGS, p. 481)

There is a counter-argument that may exist for Sikhs. The quotes above talk about the 'human being' being cast into the womb or being preserved in the womb. Stem cell research, therapeutic cloning and IVF involve embryos being created outside the womb in vitro. So can we assume that a soul would not be cast into an embryo unless it existed in utero? In this case, the issue shifts to the status of an embryo as a potential person. That is, all embryos, whether created inside or outside the body, have the potential to exhibit the properties of a human being if allowed to develop and fulfil their potential, and therefore are worthy of respect. However, this leads to a further question, what if it ever becomes possible with technology for human embryos to develop without ever being transferred to a woman? Therefore, for most Sikhs the issue of potentiality does not arise; divine law or process dictates that ensoulment (the condition for being a person) occurs at the point of fertilization of the egg by the sperm, whether occurring inside or outside the body. This ensouled embryo is a divine gift, a stage of a human being's life in which he/she is unattached from ego and therefore in direct communion with God. In return God provides succour to prepare it for the world. The time spent in the womb (as an embryo/foetus) is a valuable element of the spiritual development of the human being:

Through the union of mother and father, the fetus is formed. The egg and sperm join together to make the body.
Upside-down within the womb, it lovingly dwells on the Lord; God provides for it, and gives it nourishment there. (GGS, p. 1,013)

The Concept of Marriage and Family in Sikhism and the Ethics of ART

The use of ART will often result in children being created from the genetic material of a third party donor with whom they have no relationship once they are born. This raises fundamental questions around the concept of marriage and family within Sikhism and the role of the biological parents.

In Sikhism, marriage is a key requirement for both spiritual development and society as a whole. For Sikhs, marriage and conception are a sacred act blessed in front of the Guru Granth Sahib.

Sikhism rejects asceticism; renunciation of worldly life, celibacy or the separation from one's family or home to achieve union with God. Married life, *grihasta*, is celebrated and encouraged.

The family is a holy institution and not just an organization that emerged as a result of a social contract. It is written in the Guru Granth Sahib that

> Mother, father, progeny – are all God's creation.
> All by God in relationship are joined. (GGS, p. 494)

The fifth Guru, Guru Arjan Dev, asserts:

> Mother, father, wife and progeny, relations, loved ones and brother
> By good fortune acquired in previous births have met. (GGS, p. 700)

It may be noted from the above verses that the doctrine of transmigration, like all other Indian religions, form an inseparable part of the Sikh view. Even our family relations are determined by God according to our past doings. But more than advocating any predeterminism, the Guru Granth Sahib seems to emphasize the holy character and purpose of the institution of the family.

In artificial insemination, the process of using the sperm of a donor, rather than of a husband, presents a number of ethical issues. Insemination by the sperm of the husband would generally be viewed as using medical technology to aid the reproductive process between a man and woman within the confines of a marriage. There may be a question of whether the couple are interfering with God's will or *hukam* by 'creating' a child even though God has not willed it in the marriage. However, the counterargument would run that God has given humanity an intellect to use it for beneficial purposes, which includes medical treatment, so long as it does not harm other living creatures in the process. In practice, Sikhs would probably not see any moral difference between a child conceived through natural means and one conceived through artificial insemination of the husband's sperm into the wife's womb.

Difficult ethical issues do arise when using the sperm of a third party, further complicated when comparing the sperm donation from a relative or from an unrelated or anonymous donor.

In Sikhism, having a child within a married relationship is paramount to the welfare of the child and his/her successful functioning within the community. Hence it could be argued that conception within a married relationship, even using the sperm of another man, fulfils this requirement so long as both the husband and wife are happy to go along this path. However, Sikhs would raise a series of objections to this method, as derived from the Sikh teachings. As stated above, insemination using the husband's sperm would generally be seen as permissible and acceptable. When the sperm of another man is used there are a number of problematic issues that may arise. The insemination of a wife with the sperm of someone other than her husband could be viewed as only one step removed from adultery and consequently an adultery-like stigma is attached to the process. The child will not have the genetic material from the father who will care for it, which confuses issues of kinship and threatens the sanctity of the family's genetic lineage. Simultaneously, the third party is contributing his genetic material to the child without any due regard or responsibility for its upbringing. Even with the consent of the husband and the anonymity of the donor, it could be argued that a man's relationship with a child conceived through such intervention may not be as strong as if he were the biological father. There may also be feelings of inadequacy and jealousy that might put the marriage and family at risk in the long term. The change in 2005 of the United Kingdom's law concerning the anonymity of the donor is another factor that would have to be seriously considered as being able to cause disruption in a family unit when the child reaches eighteen years.

In practice it is not known how many Sikh couples have undergone the artificial insemination procedure or will choose to in the future. For those that do, a secondary issue arises about the identity, race and religion of the sperm donor. If a Sikh couple were to go ahead with sperm from a donor, it is likely that they would want the donor to be Sikh and probably of the same caste as them. Sikhs believe you are born into a religion and have a loose hereditary principle of faith. Many Sikhs also have strong bonds to their caste. However, it is unlikely that couples in the West would be able to obtain sperm from a donor who exactly matches their strict racial and religious requirements. Hence, a

Sikh couple would probably be prepared to consider a donor of a different faith or no faith but of a similar racial make-up to themselves so the child could 'blend' into the family and community as best as possible. It should be noted that many Sikh couples would wish to keep the matter as confidential as possible to avoid any criticism or comments from the family or community. Many Sikh couples may end up turning to India for a source of suitable donors.

On the whole, analysis of Sikh scripture suggests that Sikhism would prohibit artificial insemination using sperm from a donor other than the husband. This type of insemination would result in issues around adultery, inheritance and family disharmony. It also relinquishes the biological father of any responsibility for the child he has helped to create, which goes against Sikh teaching.

If the husband is infertile, then all possible modes of medical help should be explored to help the couple conceive without compromizing the sacred bonds of marriage. If this fails, then adoption could be considered. It has been custom in Punjabi communities for a childless couple to adopt nieces or nephews although admittedly this will diminish in the future as family sizes generally become smaller.

To conclude this section I would like to consider another scenario around artificial insemination and how Sikhs may deal with it. Consider a widow who wants to have a child using her own eggs but sperm (from a sperm bank) that her terminally ill husband donated while alive, with the knowledge that it may be used after he dies.[4] There are a number of issues here. First, as the husband has died, some may argue that if the husband is dead, then one should not interfere with God's will. Second, a child will be born knowingly without a father and, strictly speaking, not within a marriage. In other words, the father is contributing his genetic material to the child but will not directly participate in the upbringing of that child, thereby neglecting the need of the child for a father. However, generally, Sikhs would be sympathetic to the woman in this case. Consent of the husband has been obtained and the husband is indirectly providing for the child through any wealth he has left behind. The sanctity of genetic lineage is maintained and, overall, the wife would be seen as morally correct in fulfilling her dead husband's last request of having a child. If the widow were to remarry, this would cast doubt and present other ethical issues over the decision to have this child, however.

Conclusion

As science progresses and begins to provide evidence-based answers and theories about the origins of the universe and humanity, answers based on belief and faith increasingly come under scrutiny. Up to now, Sikhs have generally not engaged in such discussion but will increasingly be asked to do so, particularly in Western countries. In terms of the origin of the universe and the position of human beings in creation, there is a large disconnect between science and Sikhism. Sikhism, like other major faith traditions, invokes the need for a divine source of creation and believes that humanity sits at the apex of creation. Science does not subscribe to this view. It is unlikely or impossible that science and religion can ever be reconciled, but for Sikhs this does not appear to be a problem, as they are seen as two distinct systems which are attempting to answer different questions.

Of more pressing and practical concern to Sikhs are the ethics around biomedical technology. There is no definitive or blanket answer to the acceptability of using egg or sperm donation, IVF or assisted reproductive technology. Such advances in biology and medicine have been created by God's will and present new challenges to Sikhs in terms of interpreting scriptures and teachings to form a consensus on these issues. This is because the sacred scriptures and the Sikh code of conduct only provide guidance on general matters and one can only extrapolate these teachings to cover the new developments. Such discussions trigger lively debates among Sikhs and as yet no clear consensus has emerged. As a result, most Sikhs will continue to make a personal choice on these matters. Interpretation of Sikh scripture would suggest that processes in which embryos are wilfully destroyed or where a child is conceived from the egg or sperm of donors is morally wrong. However, to many Sikhs the use of IVF or egg and sperm donation is currently an entirely personal matter and will continue to be so until the Sikh code of conduct starts to address these issues.

Chapter 3

Sikhism and Women

Introduction

> In all beings is he himself pervasive. Himself pervades all forms male and female. (GGS, p. 605)
>
> Women and men, all the men and women, all came from the One Primal Lord God. (GGS, p. 983)

The above quotes taken from the Guru Granth Sahib, the source of all spirituality for Sikhs, indicate that God sees no difference between male and female form. But how far do Sikh teachings emphasize an equality between women and men, and how do Sikhs define this equality? It has been claimed that gender equality is a basic postulate of the Sikh faith since, 'from mother's blood and father's semen is created the human form' (GGS, p. 1,022). Whenever gender equality is discussed, the following verse from Guru Nanak is cited:

> From woman, man is born; within woman, man is conceived; to woman he is engaged and married.
> Woman becomes his friend; through woman, the future generations come.
> When his woman dies, he seeks another woman; to woman he is bound.
> So why call her bad? From her, kings are born. From woman, woman is born; without woman, there would be no one at all.
> O Nanak, only the True Lord is without a woman.
> That mouth which praises the Lord continually is blessed and beautiful.

O Nanak, those faces shall be radiant in the Court of the True Lord. (GGS, p. 473)

It is also argued that equality is accorded to women because the Guru Granth Sahib contains feminine symbolism and gives women a prominent role in the sacred and secular realms (Nikky Singh 1993). This chapter seeks to answer three questions: (1) Did the Gurus raise the position of women? (2) How did the Sikh conception of equality, which emerged against a background of Mughal and Hindu social stratification, evolve? (3) How has it developed in contemporary Sikh social life in India and the diaspora?

For centuries the status of women in India was systematically downgraded, not only through the doctrine that was present in the religious texts, but also in the social environment, and especially through the institution of the family. The second-class status was based on these religions' beliefs about the role of men and the place of women in a divinely ordered universe (Banerjee 1983, Kaur 1990, Pinkham 1967, Singh 1993).

Literature at the time of the Gurus did not focus on how women contributed to the well-being of society. Instead, the focus was on how men feared and oppressed women because they believed that women distracted men from their religious calling. Manu, the Hindu lawgiver (second century CE), justified these religious sanctions:

A girl, by a young woman, or even by an aged one, must do nothing independently, even in her own house. In childhood a female must be subject to her father, in youth to her husband, when her lord (husband) is dead to her sons; a woman must never be independent. She must not seek to separate herself from her father, husbands, or sons; by leaving them she would make both her own and her husband's families contemptible. (Olivelle 2004, Code of Manu 5, pp. 147–9)

Manu went to the point of declaring that the service of the husband by the woman is considered to be equal to the service of God (Doniger and Smith 1991):

Though he is destitute of virtue, or seeking pleasure elsewhere, or devoid of good qualities, yet a faithful wife must constantly worship a husband as god. No sacrifice, no vow, no fast must be performed by women apart from their husbands; if a wife obeys her husband, she will for that reason alone be exalted in heaven. (Olivelle 2004, Code of Conduct 5, p. 155)

As per Manu's laws only a male could perform the last rites and death anniversaries (*saradhas*) for the dead. Inheritance of the family's property was also limited to males and dowry was prevalent. Men could be polygamous whereas women were supposed to burn themselves alive on the funeral pyre of their dead husbands (*sati*). A male child was preferred since he alone could carry his father's name whereas a woman's name (both first and last) were changed at marriage when the woman became the property of her husband's family. Education of women was looked down upon. Women were only allowed to do household work and hence became economically dependent on men, and as a consequence they were considered to be the property of men. While the religion of Islam advanced the cause of women from pre-Mohammed times, it too gives man guardianship over woman. The value on this property was assigned based on the type of service women could render to men. Further, a female was viewed as the great temptress/seducer distracting men from the spiritual path, and thus could not be trusted and needed to be controlled.

Family Life

When Guru Nanak appeared on the scene, reformers such as Kabir had begun to make inroads against ritualism, hierarchy and caste in religion. Guru Nanak was able to consolidate the teachings of these reformers and through his own spiritual experiences blend them with his own unique philosophy. He emphasized the oneness of mankind and the fact that spiritual liberation was open to all regardless of caste, race or gender (Cole and Sambhi 1985, Khuswant Singh 1991). This went against the orthodox religious philosophies and practices of the time. As a result of his approach to religion and sprituality, Guru Nanak removed obstacles that other religious traditions believed prevented sprituality, such as family. This in turn raised the position of women and reestablished the family, which had been destroyed by the various traditional beliefs that religious life had to be separated from family life. While celibacy and asceticism, which by implication negate equality, was celebrated in Hinduism it was not looked highly upon in Sikhism. The traditional Hindu scheme of *Varna* and *Ashrama* (four stages of life: student, householder, elder and recluse/monk) came to be rejected in Sikhism. According to Guru Nanak, it was only by 'living amid wife and children that one would attain release' (GGS, p. 661). A truly religious person did not retire from the world but 'battled in the open field, with one's mind perfectly in control and with one's heart poised in love, all the time' (GGS, p. 931). Thus, married life, *grihasta*, was celebrated to restore women to their due place and status as an equal in life and in the spiritual quest (Singh 1993, p. 31). [1]

Bhai Gurdas, the earliest exponent of the message of Guru Granth Sahib emphasized the importance of household religion:

As the sea is the greatest among the ponds and the rivers
And summer is most respected among the mountains.
As the sandalwood tree is costly among the trees,
Gold is regarded as precious among metals.
(As) swan is most virtuous among the birds,
Lion is mightiest amongst the animals.
(As) Sri Rag is primary among the musical measures,
Touchstone is precious among the stones
(As) knowledge of the Guru is supreme amongst various forms of knowledge
(And) Contemplation of Guru is (most rewarding)
Amongst forms of Contemplation
Similarly the religion of the household is supreme among the religions. (GGS, p. 376)

Guru Amar Das appreciated the householder's life for through it one can practise charity and serve the needs of the others:

Better than the ascetic pose is the householder's life
Wherein is practised charity. (GGS, p. 587)

Again, the Guru says that the recluse leaves the household life but fails to control his desires for the world. Thus, he loses both:

Leaving progeny as man turns recluse,
His mind still is fired with desire.

While by desire gripped, realization he does not get;
By the Master's Word turning desire less joy he obtains.
(GGS, p. 835)

Thus, for the Gurus it was essential that one followed the path of the householder to achieve spiritual liberation:

Those who meditate on God attain salvation. For them, the cycle of birth and death is eliminated. (GGS, p. 11)

He has given you a body, wealth, property, peace and beautiful mansions. Nanak says, listen mind: why don't you remember God and meditate on Him? The Lord is the provider of all peace and comfort. There is no other at all. Nanak says, listen mind: salvation is attained by meditating on Him. (GGS, p. 1,426)

Thus, unlike other Indian religions, family life in Sikhism came to be recognized as a sanctified life. When Guru Nanak was questioned by the *Sidhas* as to why he, a religious preacher, 'added yeast to milk', by leading a married life, the Guru replied, 'Even you have not achieved what you preach, otherwise why would you denounce women and yet go begging to them for food'.

A learned questioner asked the same question from Guru Hargobind, who not only led a family life but also wore two swords (*miri/piri*). The Guru's reply was

Money is my servant. Wife is my conscience and children keep the race going. (GGS, p. 1,005)

The institution of family became the centre of religious as well as secular affairs and activities. However, the institution of family as perceived in Sikhism is not an end in itself but a means to attain the ultimate goal of human life, which is deliverance from the cycle of transmigration. Thus, family becomes a holy institution and not just an organization that emerged as a result of a social contract. Regarding the family Guru Amar Das writes,

Mother, father, progeny – all are God's creation.
All by God in relationships are joined. (GGS, p. 494)

Guru Arjan Dev also reasserts:

Mother, father, wife, progeny, relations,
Loved friends and brothers
By good fortune acquired in previous births have met. (GGS, p. 700)

The above highlight that God determines even family relations according to one's past doings. But more than advocating any predetermination, the Guru seems to emphasize the holy character and purpose of the institution of the family. Through the institution of the family the doctrine of liberated-in-life can be achieved. Individual as well as collective liberation is promoted:

On the Name Divine with thy heard meditate ever;
Thereby to your companions and associates liberation you bring.
(GGS, p. 394)

The Guru further holds:

Blessed is the birth of the servant of God,
Whom the Lord, rewarder of deeds, with Progeny has furnishes
Along with him all assembled groups attain liberation. (GGS, p. 532)

Having repudiated the Hindu degradation of women, which was evident in the rules to achieve union with God (celibacy), it is important to note that although the family in the hymns of the Sikh Gurus is conceived of as an ideal institution for interaction between the individual and society, attachment to family was also considered to be an obstacle in the way of God realization. Although the institution of renunciation in its traditional sense, such as leaving one's family to become spiritual and achieve salvation, came to be disregarded, there was an element of renunciation, which was integrated within household religion, which, through the process of internal reorientation, involved prayer and *sewa* (service). A Sikh while living as a person-in-the world internally had to remain detached amidst attachments:

By power of the Master's word flee doubt and fear;
Such a one engaged though in household affairs
Yet remains unattached. (GGS, p. 1,070)

Guru Amar Das writes:

By contemplation of holy truth is self-illuminated;
Thereby even in attachment to pleasure of the world one
unattached remains.
Such is the holy Preceptor's great miracle,

That even living with progeny and wife man the supreme state attains. (GGS, p. 661)

Bhai Gurdas writes:

Seeing his son, wife and relatives, he should not be ensnared by attachment, and refrain from fraud and coercion. (GGS, p. 11)

Bard Kirat also expresses similar views:

Full of demerits are we, without a single merit,
Discarding Amrita, poison we swallow.
Deluded by *Maya* – attachment and doubt
To progeny and wife are we attached. (GGS, p. 1,406)

In Sikhism, the lotus (Sanskrit: *padma*) primarily represents beauty and non-attachment. The lotus is rooted in the mud but floats on the water without becoming wet or muddy. For Sikhs it symbolizes how one should live in the world in order to gain release from rebirth: without attachment to one's surroundings (Singh 2006, pp. 142–3):

As the lotus flower floats unaffected in the water, so does he remain detached in his own household. (GGS, p. 949)
In his own home, he remains unattached, like the lotus flower in the water. (GGS, p. 1,070)
The lotus flower is with the scum and the water, but it remains untouched by any pollution. (GGS, p. 990)

Family, therefore, provides an ideal place for practising social as well as religious duties and obligations. But when the family itself becomes the goal through attachment to and greed for temporary worldly comforts, it turns into an obstacle on the pathway to the realization of the ultimate goal (Lahori 1985). It is because of attachment to the family and children that one indulges in corrupt and dishonest practices, and as a result becomes an obstacle in the realization of an ideal life. As individuals Sikhs have to realize that the stay in this world is not permanent:

I respectfully bow to those who live like a guest in this temporary world.
Such persons are honoured both in this world and in God's court.

(GGS: Bhai Gurdas Varan, p. 12:3)

Thus, the Gurus repudiated the Hindu degradation of women, which was evident in their rules on renunciation. Instead, the Gurus argued that man and woman could both achieve spiritual liberation through prayer and *sewa* while living the life of a householder.

Purdah

The Gurus also raised their voices against individual inequities against women. For example, women were mythicized as the agent of sin and evil. They distracted men from their spiritual quest through their beauty. *Purdah (veil)* was a custom strictly enforced among women for two reasons (Singh 2000). First, women needed to be covered because they were viewed as 'temptresses' for the celibate priests. Second, it was thought to be a protective shield for women. This indicated a relationship of distrust between the two sexes. However, for the Gurus, the veil made women anonymous and ultimately powerless. Thus, for the Gurus it was not women's fault if men were distracted by them from their spiritual question. Men had to learn to control their desires. Also, the act of wearing the veil did not make women religious. Instead, it was what they practiced, that is, *nam simran* that was important. This was stressed by Kabir:

Stay, stay, O daughter-in-law – do not cover your face with a veil.
In the end, this shall not bring you even half a shell.
The one before you used to veil her face;
Do not follow in her footsteps.
The only merit in veiling your face is
That for a few days, people will say, 'What a noble bride has come'.
Your veil shall be true only if
You skip, dance and sing the Glorious Praises of the Lord.
Says Kabeer, the soul-bride shall win,
Only if she passes her life singing the Lord's praises. (GGS, p. 484)

As a result, the wearing of veils in the *sangat* (Sikh congregation) was abolished. For example, Guru Amar Das did not allow the Queen of Haripur to come into the *sangat* (religious assembly) wearing a veil. The immediate effect of the removal of *purdah* was that a woman was no longer to be viewed as a temptress or a helpless individual who had to be suppressed, but instead as a responsible individual being endowed with a will of her own.

> False modesty that suppressed is ended.
> Now with veil cast off am I started on the way of devotion. (Guru Granth Sahib, p. 931)

Instead of wearing the veil, women, like the men, were required to cover their head only as a matter of respect.

Sati

The Gurus also prohibited the practice of *sati*, the self-immolation of widows on their husbands' funeral pyres. Again, this was a practice, which reinforced the belief that women had no identity of their own without a male (Banerjee 1983, McLeod 1997).[2] According to the Gurus, *sati* had no place in a 'God-fearing' society and no spiritual worth. Guru Amar Das who persuaded King Akbar to outlaw the practice wrote:

> Do not call her '*sati*' who burns herself with along with their husbands' corpses.
> O Nanak, they alone are known as '*sati*', who dies from the shock of separation.
> They are also known as '*sati*', who abides in modesty and contentment.
> They serve their Lord, and rise in the early hours to contemplate Him. (GGS, p. 787)

Although the practice of *sati* was forbidden and outlawed by the Gurus, and widow remarriage promoted, widows were still ostracized – They may not have been forced to die, but they were made to lead a separate life from the family (Banerjee 1983).

Active Religious Life

Pruthi and Sharma (1995) and McLeod (1989a) suggest that because the Gurus were all men, and because most significant individuals cited in the Guru Granth Sahib were men, the Gurus were supporting a patriarchal system (Singh 2006, p. 147).

While it cannot be argued that the Gurus operated within a patriarchal system, to say that they supported it is much less clear and indeed can be argued against. Guru Nanak, and the other Gurus, allowed women an equal share in political and religious life, for according to Guru Nanak,

> It is through woman that order is maintained. (GGS, p. 473)

The Gurus grounded their idealism regarding women in practical structures such as the institution of the free *langar* (community kitchen) where food was provided for all freely without any distinction of creed, caste or gender. Guru Amar Das appointed women as preachers and 22 women headed *Manjis* (political/religious units) established by the Guru. In religious worship, the Gurus eradicated the need of an intermediary, a priest, to gain access to God. Women could read and recite from the Guru Granth Sahib, and could sit in the *sangat* (congregation) with men and were given an equal right to pray and sing in the congregation, fostering values of equality. Women were given an equal right to participate in the congregation:

> Come my sisters and dear comrades! Clasp me in thine embrace.
> Meeting together, let us tell the tales of our Omnipotent Spouse (God).
> In the True Lord are all merits, in us all demerits. (GGS, p. 17)

The Gurus also stressed that it is those who repeat the praise of God who will prove acceptable, whether they be man or woman. Spiritual progress can be acquired by all through prayer and *sewa* in the realm of the family.

The uniqueness of all this was that previously women were excluded from participating in religious ceremonies. In the Hindu death rituals, for example, the son alone was permitted to light the funeral pyre. The funeral procession only consisted of men. The Hindu wedding party also consisted solely of male friends and relatives. In stark contrast to such predominantly male participation in rituals, the Sikh text reveals the centrality of women in the process of consecrating ceremonies – be they related to marriage or death.

Khalsa

Through the above the Gurus promoted values of equality between the sexes. This equality was strengthened further by the tenth Guru through the formation of the *Khalsa Panth* (The Pure Brotherhood), which was perceived as the ideal community, which was embedded in values of equality (McLeod 1968, Singh K 1991).

Men and women can be members of the *Khalsa*. Upon baptism women can wear the same five emblems of the *Khalsa* as men do. While men received the surname 'Singh', women received the surname 'Kaur', signifying princess. Thus, the patriarchal structure of society was modified (McLeod 1968). Men and women no longer traced their lineage or occupation to the father. As 'Singh' and 'Kaur', they were both equal partners in the new family. They could join the *Panj Pyare* (Five Beloved Ones), become priests, perform *kirtan* and solemnize marriages. Women embraced this equality in religious life, and Sikh women played a decisive role in the formation of the *Khalsa Panth*. Two women who took up this freedom and newfound status at the time of the Gurus were Mata Sahib Kaur and Mai Bhago.

Mata Sahib Kaur – The Mother of the *Khalsa*

The importance of women participating in religious ceremonies is clearly reflected in the story of the founding of the *Khalsa*. When Guru Gobind Singh prepared *amrit* for the baptism ceremony, Mata Sahib Kaur represented women and added sugar puffs to the Holy Water.

The *Khalsa* was a martial order, but by her gesture Mata Sahib Kaur symbolically added modesty and sweetness to its traits. She is therefore known as 'The Mother of the *Khalsa*'.

Also, when Guru Gobind Singh died in 1708, Mata Sahib Kaur settled in Delhi and guided the affairs of the *Khalsa*. It was she who directed Bhai Mani Singh to collect Guru Gobind Singh's writings and edit them into what is now known as the *Dasam Granth* (Banerjee 1983).

Mai Bhago

It was the last Guru's wife who guided the young Sikh nation for forty years after the death of Guru Gobind when it was in danger of fragmenting. Guru Gobind Singh was besieged by the combined forces of the hill chiefs and Aurangzeb in the fort of Anandpur. As the siege was prolonged, the number of the Guru's supporters dwindled down to a hundred-odd people and the resistance seemed disastrous. Prompted by the promises of free passage, forty Sikhs tried to compel the Guru to abandon the fort and lay down arms. The Guru declined and instead advised them to hold on. Instead, the forty Sikhs resigned from the *Khalsa* and signed a disclaimer saying 'We reject you as our Guru and we renounce our allegiance to the *Khalsa*'.

When the forty deserters reached their villages, their wives, organized under Mai Bhago (later known as Bhag Kaur), criticized the cowardice of their husbands. Mai Bhago led them back to fight the armies of Wazir Khan of Sirhind at Khidrana (now known as Muktsar). Out of the forty deserters, only one, Mahan Singh, was alive when the Guru reached the battlefield.

Mahan Singh died in the Guru's arms with the satisfaction of having been pardoned for his transgression. The Guru blessed the forty brave fighters as *Muktas* (immortals) and the place came to be known as *Muktsar* (the Sacred Place of the Immortals) (Banerjee 1983).

Thus, through the action of these two women, and the teachings of the Gurus, women came to be regarded as equal with men, and women were expected to shoulder the responsibility for their own actions and spiritual progression.

Improving Women's Status through Imagery

Practically, the Gurus tried to improve women's position through the validation of family life, removal of *purdah* and *sati*, and the institution of the *Khalsa*. However, they also attempted to improve the position of women by dismissing the negative connotations surrounding female sexuality that Sikhism's immediate neighbouring traditions like Hinduism, Islam and Buddhism were embedded with, through a validation of the female in the religious text, which appears as something unique (Pruthi 1967, Singh 1993). Guru Nanak and his successors composed many hymns, which argued that a soul had no gender, no caste and no creed, and that it was essentially an extension of God that inhabits various shells until *mukti* (liberation) is achieved, when it will rejoin the infinite Creator:

Women and men, all came from the One Primal Lord God. (GGS, p. 983)

Natural Phenomenon

At the time of the Gurus there was a disdain for natural phenomenon and a false sense of impurity attached to menstruation and childbirth, which relegated women to a low place in the social strata of society. (Singh N 2005b and 1993).

However, this is not what the Gurus thought, and to correct the notions that women were unclean they made sure in the Guru Granth Sahib that there was positive imagery about a woman's role in society.

'The Sikh scripture does not debase or disdain the female body and does not place taboos around menstruation, childbirth or any other female functions' (Pruthi and Sharma 1995, p. 137). There is nothing inferior or abhorrent about feminine sexuality. For example, Guru Nanak rejected the superstition that a woman who gave birth to a child remained polluted for a number of days (40) and that the home in which the birth took place was similarly polluted (Singh 1993).

Blood symbolizes both life and death. Menstrual blood in particular symbolizes life and the creative process. As a result, Guru Nanak openly criticizes those who attribute pollution to women because of menstruation, and asserts,

> If one accepts the concept of impurity, then there is impurity everywhere.
> In cow-dung and wood there are worms.
> As many as are the grains of corn, none is without life.
> First, there is life in the water, by which everything else is made green.
> How can it be protected from impurity? It touches our own kitchen.
> O Nanak, impurity cannot be removed in this way; it is washed away only by spiritual wisdom. (GGS, p. 472)

Thus, for a Sikh, pollution lies in the heart and mind of the person and not in the natural process of birth, for in Sikhism the female is crucial to the origin of life. As a result, menstrual bleeding is acknowledged in Sikh thought as an essential natural process. Life begins with it. Sikh scripture is not reticent in regard to birth imagery: female body, flesh and the natural female processes are fully affirmed. Imagery of conception, gestation, giving birth and lactation are present throughout the Guru Granth (Singh 1993), and this is particularly so when discussing motherhood.

Motherhood

Teachings in the Guru Granth Sahib are life affirming and woman affirming. Motherhood is discussed throughout the Guru Granth Sahib positively. The image of the mother, for example, focuses on the creative and nurturing aspects of the transcendent, and throughout the Guru Granth Sahib, the mother is revered because she goes through the natural process of conception, gestation, and giving birth. Nikky Singh argues that

> The maternal imagery cannot be understood either as a romantic exaltation of women as mothers or as an automatic and mandatory process where women are tied down to be reproductive machines for begetting sons. . . . For me it is the germinative ocean, the formless potential which every female carries within her body. (Singh 2005a, p. 210)

The focus on the foetus and the womb 'reinforces the generative power of the mother. She is the maternal continuum, one who retrieves the primacy of birth over death, and reaffirms the union of body and mind' (Singh 2008, pp. 126–7). In this way, Sikh scripture highlights our source instead of having a narrow focus on where the end of life leads. The Guru Granth Sahib states,

> You yourself are born of the egg, from the womb, from sweat, from earth: you yourself are all the continents and all the worlds. (GGS, p. 604, Singh 2008, p. 127)

The Guru Granth Sahib is replete with images of the womb, in various contexts. The womb is celebrated as the matrix for all life and living. '[T]he womb becomes a vital space for the Divine, and the fetus functions as a symbol for cultivating Sikh morality, spirituality, and aesthetics . . . affirm[ing] the category of birth that feminist theologians, philosophers, and psychologists find so critical' (Singh 2008, pp. 124–5).

Such portrayals of birth and mother demonstrate that the Gurus recognized that women's main role is to give life and not destroy. The following verse, which focuses on the female's role as mother and wife, is revolutionary for its time because it contradicted the cultural norm of the time and recognized the importance of women:

> From woman, man is born; within woman, man is conceived; to
> woman he is engaged and married.
> Woman becomes his friend; through woman, the future
> generations come.
> When his woman dies, he seeks another woman; to woman he is
> bound.
> So why call her bad? From her, kings are born. From woman,
> woman is born; without woman, there would be no one at all.
> O Nanak, only the True Lord is without a woman.
> That mouth which praises the Lord continually is blessed and
> beautiful.
> O Nanak, those faces shall be radiant in the Court of the True
> Lord. (GGS, p. 473)

To give validation to the mother, God is referred to as mother as
well as father in the Guru Granth Sahib:

> Thou, O Lord, art my Father and Thou my Mother. Thou art the
> Giver of peace to my soul and very life. (GGS, p. 1,144)

The Gurus therefore elevated the status of a woman from someone
who was viewed as a nonentity to a creator and sustainer of the human
race for 'From woman, woman is born; without woman, there would
be no one at all' (GGS, p. 473).[3]

Bride and Groom

Throughout the Guru Granth Sahib the individual is presented as the
bride who is forever seeking union with her groom (God):

> The spouse is but one and all others are His brides.
> The false bride assumes many religious garbs.
> When the Lord stops her going into another's home, then is she
> summoned into her Lord's mansion without any let and
> hindrance.
> She is adorned with the Name and is dear to her True Lord. She
> alone is the true bride and the Lord lends her His support. (GGS,
> p. 933)

By using such imagery the 'male–female binarism' is dismissed (Singh
2006, p. 148). The use of the bride develops the nuance of intimacy

and passion in the human relationship with the Divine. For, as the bride shows, body and mind are both equally essential for the passage towards the Divine (McCormack 1985, Singh 1993):

> The self-willed *manmukh* performs religious rituals, like the unwanted bride decorating her body. (GGS, p. 31)

> The *Gurmukh* is the happy and pure soul-bride forever. She keeps her Husband Lord enshrined within her heart. (GGS: Guru Amar Das, p. 11)

> The happy and pure soul-bride is noble; she has infinite love for the Guru. (GGS: Guru Amar Das, line 12)

> O Nanak, blessed are the happy soul-brides, who are in love with their Husband Lord. (GGS, p. 51)

Thus, while in other religious traditions women did not find direct access to the Divine because it was viewed as a male experience, which had to be translated or transferred onto women, the central message of the Sikh literature is that by following the bride's example of loving devotion the gap is bridged between the Divine Reality and the individual. But her devotion does not call for renunciation and asceticism; she opens the way to the Transcendent by living fully and authentically in this world, maintaining her connections with her own self, her family, friends and nature. The walls between sacred and profane are destroyed and every aspect of daily life is imbued with spirituality. The bride leads us to our ultimately real and intrinsic self – the harmonization of self and body, the very spark or light (*joti*) that we are made up of (Singh 1993).

Thus, the Gurus made equality between women and men one of the basic postulates of the Sikh faith, and women were given priority because 'from mother's blood and father's semen is created the human form'.

Was Equality Achieved?

In a society submerged in rituals, caste and gender prejudice, and intolerance to other faiths and religions, the Gurus opened the way for sexual equality (Banerjee 1983) – for they argued there is no gender category, and that there is nothing inferior or insidious about woman. Throughout the Guru Granth Sahib the patriarchal polarization which existed in other vying religions – women and nature on the one side against men and culture on the other – was repudiated to give women greater equality – social and religious. Women were neither a hindrance nor a negative influence; women were necessary for the continuance of society and for the preservation of its ethnic structure. The teachings of the Guru Granth Sahib also transcend the inequality that was evident in other religions by describing the soul as neither male nor female and describing the whole of humanity (men and women) as the bride continually seeking divine union with God, the bridegroom. Spiritual liberation was no longer exclusive to men.

However, some would argue that the Guru Granth Sahib reinforces male dominance and patriarchy because the terminology used within it is male orientated, such as *Akal Purakh, Karta Purakh* and the imagery of the devotee being a bride yearning for the Male God in the form of a bridegroom or the mother giving birth to 'Kings' makes the Guru Granth Sahib anti-female, androcentric and patriarchal (Jakobsh 2003). One can also ask why Guru Gobind Singh did not choose a female as one of the *panj pyares*.

McLeod argued,

> The Gurus certainly conferred equal opportunity on both women and men, but it was equal opportunity of access to spiritual liberation. It was not equality in the sense that women might do everything that might be open to men. A woman's place was in the home, sheltered there by the caring and devotion of an upright husband. Patriarchy had certainly been deprived of its domineering aspects, but patriarchy was still intact. (1997, p. 243)

Indeed, it is clear that the Guru Granth Sahib reflects men's perception of and stereotypes about women's ideal behaviour; however, it is important to note that it is replete with images of mother, bride and many metaphors of feminine roles, and this was unique for the time. Thus, when considering verses from the Guru Granth Sahib we have to be careful from what perspective we are looking at it. To use a twenty-first century Western feministic paradigm to evaluate the writings of the Sikh Gurus would be wrong. We have to keep in mind the historical context that the text was written in, and that,

> The Sikh Gurus were vastly ahead of their contemporary society, and the orthodox Sikh view, as spelt out by the *Sikh Rehat*

Maryada, upholds the same position as the Gurus. (McLeod 1997, p. 242)

Present Day Context

Nikky Gurinder Kaur Singh (1993), in a modern study, calls Guru Nanak the first feminist and compares his thought with that of Rosemary Ruether (1975 and 1983), Mary Daly (1973), Carol Christ (1980 and 1985) and other feminists. She argues that the Gurus preached a revolutionary message, which accorded women equality and recognized the importance of women with reference to giving birth and life while creating a solid foundation on which they hoped future generations of Sikhs would build. However, the Sikh community has failed to do this in many ways:

> Generations of patriarchy have been programmed to fear her body, and this threat of her sexuality has kept readers and hearers from recognizing the semiotic significance of Sikh sacred verse. *Bani* permeates with female force and fecundity, but the fear and disdain of *her* presence has kept Sikhs from acknowledging female images in the poetic world of the Gurus. (Nikky Singh 2005, p. 2,008)

McLeod also argued that the Gurus' gender ideal did not take shape in society because patriarchy still prevailed and women played a secondary role in the sacred and secular domains. They were and still are defined in terms of their role as wife and mother. This is because the culture and social traditions of many North Indian cultures were so heavily ingrained within the psyche of the Sikhs that they overrode the fundamental tenets of the faith. Hence, the 'emancipatory conception postulated by their Gurus is aborted and sadly, a patriarchal structure is reproduced in the Sikh world' (Nikky Singh 2005, p. 202).

Today many Sikh women still have their place ascribed to them in society and family by male members – be they fathers, grandfathers, older brothers or brothers-in-law. There is still an unequal pressure on women in terms of upholding family honour and homemaking and child care even though they may hold down the same jobs as men.

Women in Gurdwaras

While progress has been made in certain realms, it is clear that the Sikh religious community is very much a man's world. Many of the rights given to women by the Gurus have been superficially utilized by the religious community. Take the importance of women being involved in religious activities: this was paramount to the Gurus. In particular, women's involvement in religious observance and services, which was intended to take women out into the wider community where they would have a definite and defined 'public' role as mothers and teachers of the youngsters. According to such teachings this requirement makes the Sikh religion progressive; however, representation does not equal power. Women today are excluded from various activities within religious institutions and this is related to the sexual divisions in Sikh society. Apart from a few high-profile examples, such as Bibi Jagir Kaur (some Sikhs would question whether she is a good example), women continue to be left in the margins. In gurdwaras there are relatively few women on the committees, and those that are find that their voices are rarely heard. Women preachers are also rare and essentially only cater to the female population. Nikky Singh affirms this:

> Moreover, public worship is also dominated by men. Almost always in Gurdwaras male lenses interpret the scriptural passages. Men have the privilege to touch and read the textual body during all forms of public worship. Since men conduct rituals and cere-monies, their voices and hands have seized the sacred modality of the sacred word. (Nikky Singh 2005b, p. 201)

In some gurdwaras you will not find any female *gianis* (priests) and women cannot participate in *akhand paths* (48-hour prayer reading). When *sewadars* are questioned about the absence of women in *kirtan* for example, a common reply is that 'women should stay at home and do what they are born to do, *sewa* of the family'. Opinderjit Takhar (2005) argued that women could not do such *sewa* in Guru Nanak Nishkam Sewak Jatha[4] because her respondents informed her that 'women have other duties such as preparation of the *langar* and cleaning of the gurdwara, which do not leave time for participating in the *akhand paths*' (Takhar 2005, p. 49). On the other hand, it is also important to note here that some women, especially the older women, argue that they are happy with doing *sewa* in the kitchen (Jhutti-Johal 2010). It is the younger women who seem to be more vocal and demanding in asking to be allowed to do *sewa* where traditionally they have not done it.

Many women today have the qualifications and experience, but have been historically discriminated against, barred from being part of the decision-making process in Sikh gurdwaras. This discrimination is grounded in the belief that women do not have the capability to organize and run gurdwaras. Sikh men argue that women are not in these decision-making roles (such as in gurdwara committees and service organizations), not because they should not be allowed to, but because they don't have the time, qualifications or experience to do so. However, one can argue that the reason women may not have these qualifications or experience is that they have historically been barred from access to opportunities that would enable them to gain skills that are required in the context of Sikh organizations. This is a Catch 22 situation, which needs to be broken.

However, it is important to note that the above assertions or arguments for why women are not in leadership roles are made invalid when we hear of instances of women taking control of gurdwaras. This was done in Coventry, Leicester, Birmingham and London where women took over the running of gurdwaras when rival factions developed in the all-male committees:

Guru Nanak Gurdwara, Smethwick, was managed by local women during 1981–2; Guru Tegh Bahadur gurdwara, Leicester, which had no elections for nine years, was also taken over by women. The Shepherd's Bush Gurdwara, when faced with a crisis as a result of rivalry between two factions, delegated charge to an all-women's committee in March 1983. (Singh and Tatla 2006, p. 85)

Case Study – The Harmandar Sahib

While gender divisions in most gurdwaras may be taken for granted, it is quite noticeable in the Harmandar Sahib (Golden Temple), the most visible and visited place of worship for Sikhs. Here Sikh women are not allowed to read from the Guru Granth Sahib, play *kirtan* or perform any *sewa* in the sanctum sanctorum (main prayer room). These *sewas* are 'reserved' for men only.

Amritdhari and non-*amritdhari* women are prevented from following the *palki* (palanquin) down the walkway, even if they are far behind the crowd. Women are asked by the men to move into the narrow median between the incoming and outgoing paths of the walkway, or are made to stand in the outgoing path. However, at the *parkash* ceremony non-*amritdhari* men, wearing scarves, can take part in the procession and hold the *palki* or wait in the queue. The problem of this discrimination against Sikh women at the Harmandar Sahib came to light in 2003 when two *amritdhari* Sikh women, Mejinderpal Kaur and Lakhbir Kaur, claimed that they were prevented by SGPC *sewadars* from participating in the *sewa* of the procession of the Guru Granth Sahib from the Darbar Sahib. The *sewadars* attending to the procession prevented them from queuing with the male members of the congregation. The *sewadars* said that they could not touch the *palki sahib* (palanquin), let alone carry it. They were told that only male members were allowed to do so.[5]

Such action worked against the policy introduced by Bibi Jagir Kaur who, after taking over as SGPC chief in 1999, had announced that baptized women could undertake religious duties in the Harmandar Sahib. Prior to Bibi Jagir Kaur, the then acting Jathedar of the *Akal Takht*, Professor Manjit Singh had taken a *Jatha* (group) of baptized women (Bibi Inderjit Kaur, the wife of Harbhajan Singh Yogi) to perform *sewa* in the sanctum sanctorum. The *sewadars'* action also contradicted Jathedar Joginder Singh's statement made in London in December 2002 where he stated that Sikh women had every right to perform *sewa* at the Harmandar Sahib.

Although Bibi Jagir Kaur, the first female president of the SGPC, passed a bill in 2005 saying that women could do such service in the Harmandar Sahib, in the same year, the five priests of Harmandar Sahib, Gyani Gurbachan Singh, Gyani Mohan Singh, Gyani Jaswinder Singh, Gyani Jagtar Singh and Gyani Mal Singh, rejected Bibi Jagbir Kaur's (SCPC Chief) request to allow baptized Sikh women to perform religious service in the inner sanctum. To date it is clear from investigations that women are still encountering problems and cannot perform *sewa*, which goes against the Sikh religion. Reasons given for why women cannot take part in the *Sukhasan* ceremony at the Harmandar Sahib (the taking of Guru Granth Sahib to the Akal Takht in the evening) include (1) women distract men from their work, that is, by their beauty or men's uncontrollable urges, and (2) they are polluting due to menstruation. Thus, it is clear from this that notions of women being polluting still do exist among the Sikh community. As Opinderjit Takhar argues, we cannot be sure of the extent to which such thinking exists, but she highlights that in some places, such as Guru Nanak Nishkam Sewak Jatha, Birmingham, menstruating women cannot take part in the cooking of food as a whole, or in the preparation of the *karah prasad*

(2005, p. 50). Such actions go against the teachings of the *gurbani* (the writings of the Gurus as found in the Sikh holy scriptures) and the *Rehat Maryada*.

However, it is important to note that when religious priests are asked why women are excluded, the common response seems to be that their exclusion from certain activities is not due to a strict code of pollution and to men's fear of distraction. Instead, they argue that 'this is always how it has been done and that there are, good practical reasons for not having women performing certain activities'. When probed what these reasons may be there are usually no further explanations. Nevertheless, whatever the explanations, contradictions exist between the religious teachings and what happens on the ground, that is, the social and religious discrimination of women.

Khalsa Women – *Panj Pyare*

The *panj pyare* or the five beloved ones are held in the highest esteem in Sikh tradition. They were the first members to join the *Khalsa* and responded to a call from Guru Gobind Singh for the heads of five worthy individuals to join his new order of saint soldiers. They represent the body of the *Khalsa* and are the embodiment of its ideals, namely equality, brotherhood and devotion. Today, the tradition of using *panj pyare* in all key Sikh ceremonies such as *Nagar Kirtans* and *amrit* continues, and their presence represents a holy congregation.

In line with the original Baisakhi ceremony, the *panj pyare* chosen to participate in ceremonies today generally tend to be male, the justification being that Guru Gobind Singh chose five men and therefore that decision should continue today. However, this presents a problem to the notion of equality within the *Khalsa*. Many women feel they should be represented in the *panj pyare* since it is such an important institution, which should represent the whole of the Sikh community, not just its male members.

However, women find it difficult, if not impossible to be one of the *panj pyare*. Yogi Bhajan's 3HO (Healthy, Happy, Holy Organization) organization is the only one that allows women to be part of the *panj pyare*. They argue that for them the *Khalsa* has no gender and the *panj pyare* can be any five Sikhs of the Guru, not any five men of the Guru.

Thus, although the Guru Granth Sahib and the Sikh *Rehat Maryada* do not prohibit women from taking part in religious services and leading prayers, it is clear that there is some form of gender discrimination going on in many gurdwaras with reference to the activities that women can participate in, both in Punjab and in the diaspora. As a result of this discrimination, women have been confined to the private sphere, while men have been given access to the religious, which is justified on the grounds that this is how it has always been.

Dowry

Paying and accepting dowry (*daj*), a centuries-old South Asian tradition where the bride's parents present gifts of cash, clothes and jewellery to the groom's family at a wedding, was condemned by the Gurus:

> Any other dowry, which the perverse place for show that is false pride and worthless gilding. O' my Father! Give me the Name of Lord God as a gift and dowry. (GGS, p. 79)

Although the practice was condemned by the Gurus and was made illegal in India in 1961, it is still prevalent today and has not been curbed. As a consequence girls are seen as a financial burden and an economic liability. This perception has contributed to the rise in female foeticide.

Although dowry is supposed to be a voluntary gift, it is often demanded from the parents of the girls (Sen 2002). There has been an escalation in dowry abuse and violence over the last decade in the West and in Punjab. Demands made by potential in-laws before a marriage, and even after marriage, demonstrate that they have no respect for the woman as an individual in her own right but are instead more concerned with money and what they can get out of the woman and her family (Bhachu 1985, Jhutti 1998). For example, in Punjab, Maruti cars, motorbikes, farm equipment and gold are demanded and in most instances are given to the groom and his extended family. In the United Kingdom there have been weddings where demands have been made and parents have had to take out second mortgages on their homes to fund the demands (Jhutti 1998).[6]

In Indian media it is very common to read about 'kitchen fires' (Sen M 2002), an Indian euphemism for the murder of the bride if the husband's parents were dissatisfied with the motor scooter or refrigerator delivered by the bride's parents. While 'kitchen fires' or bride burning are common in India, and although this is not heard of in the United Kingdom, it is clear from the number of domestic violence cases being reported to the authorities and cases coming before the court[7] that dowry plays a role in this violence. As a result in the West, dowry abuse is viewed as a cultural form of domestic violence.

The increasing incident of dowry abuse amongst the Sikh and Hindu communities in the United Kingdom has led the Labour MP for Ealing Southall in London, Virendra Sharma, to call for a similar law to one that exists in India (Dowry Prohibition Act 1961) to be introduced in the United Kingdom. Although Virendra Sharma may lobby for an anti-dowry law, in an attempt to curb the problem it has to be kept in mind that in India the dowry system continues to thrive despite the ban[8] (Poonam Taneja [BBC Asian Network]: MP demands law against dowries, accessed 30 October 2009 (http://news.bbc.co.uk/1/hi/uk/8093948.stm).

It is because of such abuse that the birth of a daughter is viewed negatively. One 65-year-old gentleman told me:

As soon as my daughter was born I started saving for her dowry. I had two daughters and for each I had a bank account from when they were born in which I used to put money every week.

While in the past the burden of saving for a dowry was on the parents, today, due to education, women are financially independent and pro-fessionally successful and thus contribute to their dowry, and therefore cannot be viewed as a burden on their parents or on their husband's family. Nevertheless, the financial independence that they have gained through employment is also contributing to the dowry abuse. By com-piling large dowries, women have created problems for themselves. The expectation for larger and larger dowries keeps growing (Bhachu 1985 and 1986, Jhutti 1998).

Female Foeticide

Although the Gurus had tried to eradicate the negative perceptions surrounding daughters, it is clear that today sons continue to be val-ued more than daughters in the Sikh community. A son is viewed as an asset, while a daughter is perceived to be a liability. A son is viewed as the inheritor of the family name and wealth and is able to provide for the family and continue the family line, whereas a daughter is a drain on family resources due to education and dowry and will eventually belong to the family of her future husband (Menski 1998).

Female mortality (in infancy) that was prevalent at the time of the Gurus has been replaced today by female foeticide[9] (see Chapter 4). Sikh religious teachings do not support female foeticide, which I also define as abortion, but condemns it because it is the destruction of a living soul. However, it is undeniable that with the advent of scientific technology members of the Sikh community engage in the practices of female foetal abortion and gender pre-selection. This is evidenced by the male to female ratio in Punjab (see Chapter 4).

A study published in the British medical journal *Lancet* (Pabha at Jha et al. 2006, pp. 211–18, 367) found the boy–girl ratio changed markedly after the introduction of ultrasound technology that was intended to diagnose foetal abnormalities and illnesses. Technological advancement that was supposed to improve the mortality rate and health of children is being used to identify the sex of a child before it is born and is leading to the gradual decline in the number of female births. The most dramatic decline of female births came between 1991 and 2001, from 945 girls for every 1,000 boys to 927. This is despite the introduction of a ban in India in 1994 on sex-selective abortions.[10]

According to India's 2001 Census Haryana had 819 girls (per 1,000 boys), Delhi 868, Gujarat 883 and the worst example was the northern state of Punjab with one of the worst gender ratios at 798 girls to 1,000 boys (www.censusindia.net/t_00_003.html, accessed 21 October 2009).

As a result of these figures the Akal Takht, the highest seat of political and spiritual power of Sikhs, used the *Rehat Maryada* of 1950, which recommends the total ostracization of such a person and family from society:

(l) A Sikh should not kill his daughter; nor should he maintain any relationship with a killer of a daughter (SGPC 1950),[11]

to issue a *Hukumnama* (edict) on 18 April 2001. The edict stated that any Sikh aborting a female foetus would be excommunicated as the practice was forbidden under *Rehat Maryada*:

The Jathedar of Sri Akal Takht Sahib, Giani Joginder Singh to raise the status of women in the religious community said: To put an end to this inhuman, immoral and irreligious practice, in the light of Gurmat thought and philosophy, the Five Singh *Sahibans* from the portals of Akal Takht Sahib order all Guru

Nanak *Naam Levas* that no Gurmukh man or woman, on detection of a female child in the womb, should resort to the Manmukhi act of female foeticide. Any person doing so is a *Tankhaiya*. We also appeal to humankind that we should respect the individuality of every person rising above gender considerations.

Despite the *Hukumnama* being passed in 2001 the practice still continues today. This is evidenced by two things: first, the conference held in Amritsar five years later on 23 April 2006, by the Shiromani Gurdwara Prabandhak Committee (SGPC) in collaboration with UNESCO titled 'Basic Human Dignity: Foeticide and Violence Against Women'.

Second, a study published in 2007 by Dr Dubuc arguing that Indian women in the United Kingdom are aborting unborn daughters. Dr Dubuc suggests that between 1990 and 2005 1,500 girls were 'missing' from English and Welsh birth statistics. The report also highlights that the proportion of boys born to Indian-born mothers compared with girls has increased since the 1970s and this could be due to 'sex selective abortion' (2007). As a consequence of this in the United Kingdom certain NHS Trusts stopped telling Asian parents, whether Sikh, Hindu or Muslim, the sex of their foetus. However, Asian couples have got around this by going to India and having the scan there, and if need be an abortion if the foetus is female.

Thus, these figures for India and the United Kingdom, and the apparent involvement of the Sikh religious authorities in trying to curb this problem, clearly highlight that there is immense pressure to have a male child. Today, if the first child born to a married couple is a girl, while most of the family will be happy that the child is healthy, the pressure that the next child is a boy increases. Remarks such as 'having a mixed family would have been nice' on the birth of another girl disguises the preference for boys. No one says this if the couple have two boys.

Although recent research suggests that the younger generation seems far less worried about the sex of their children, they are still confronted by pressure from the older generation of the extended family. However, it needs to be noted whether younger couples use the argument that the 'older generation are pressuring them' as a cover for their own preference for a male child. Or are we really seeing a shift in mentality? Current research (Jha Prabhat 2006, Sen 2003) seems to suggest that growing economic prosperity and education levels have not led to a corresponding mitigation as far as reducing female foeticide is concerned. While the ratio had been declining up until 2001, it will be interesting to see what figures from the 2011 India Census will show after such intervention from the state and religious organizations in attempting to curb the problem.

Consequence: Shortage of Marriageable Women

It is also important to note that the consequence of female foeticide will be a shortage of marriageable women in the future. The cultural preference for boys is creating an artificial disparity between the number of boys and girls. Terminating female foetuses will eventually lead to a shortage in the number of marriageable Sikh women and this will inevitably lead to people marrying out of their religion and caste. The consequence of this is that the bloodline of the Sikhs will become diluted and this is what the Sikh community wants to prevent through the enforcement of marrying within one's religion and caste.

On the other hand, the lack of women of marriageable age will also mean that in 10 to 15 years parents will not be able to find Sikh wives for their sons, and the parents of girls of marriageable age will be able to pick and choose a groom for their daughter. In fact, it could be argued that there may even be a scenario where the boy's family will have to pay the girl's family a 'reverse dowry'. Thus, the long-term consequence of female foeticide may inadvertently help improve the quality of life for women and bring boys and girls to an equal footing.

Conclusion

Although the issue of gender inequality is a global one, it is clear from the Sikh Gurus' egalitarian ideal that their theology was inclusive with its emphasis on social as well as religious equality. McLeod (1997, p. 242) stresses how Guru Nanak's teachings regarding gender 'carry us well beyond the conventional view of his time or, for that matter, the present time as well'. However, it is evident from current research that complete equality for women has not been achieved for the Sikh religious community and it is still very much a man's world.

Some, like Pruthi and Sharma (1995) and McLeod (1997), suggest that equality has not been achieved because the Gurus were all men, and the most significant individuals cited in the Guru Granth Sahib were men, therefore the Gurus were supporting a patriarchal system (Singh G 2006, p. 147).

The Gurus' religious ideal has also not been achieved due to Indian traditional and cultural practices, which have become merged with religious practice and enforce gender inequality. For example, culturally, Sikhs have shown a preference for sons. This preference has been reinforced by both an intensely patriarchal mindset and the dowry system, and as a consequence has promoted gender inequality.

Chapter 4

Sikhism and Ethics

Introduction

Sikh moral and ethical values are based on the idea of *natural law* – similar to the Roman Catholic idea of natural law – the way God wants the universe to work. The Gurus engaged in discussions about matters such as obligations to society, to family and to God. These dialogues promoted strong ethical and moral values, which guided followers on how to live and behave in this world if they wished to achieve liberation from the cycle of birth and rebirth.

Moral and ethical values that emanated from the time of the Gurus, which are contained in stories and hymns within the Guru Granth Sahib, *Dasam Granth*, compositions of Bhai Gurdas, *Janam-sakhis* and *Rahit-namas*, have been handed down from generation to generation and have been interpreted and formalized in the 1950 *Rehat Maryada* (Code of Conduct), which provides guidance on religious matters. These values have generally been adhered to but are being tested within the modern era causing changes to take place in the realm of Sikh ethics and morality. This chapter will endeavour, through an analysis of scripture, to look at what moral and ethical living meant at the time of the Gurus and what it means today. This will be discussed alongside ethnographic research from Britain and India to highlight the dichotomy between conservative and liberal religious discourse. The first section of this chapter looks at how the Sikh Gurus wanted Sikhs to live among fellow Sikhs and within the wider community of non-Sikhs. The concepts of social responsibility will be discussed, as will the social institutions of marriage and family. The second section of this chapter will address new ethical and moral issues that are confronting Sikhs today, such as the moral status of the foetus, contraception, abortion, homosexuality, death and euthanasia, all of which are having an impact on Sikh notions of morality and ethics today, and discuss how religion affects and is affected by contemporary society. These modern-day issues will be addressed through an analysis of religious teachings contained within the Guru Granth Sahib to assess how this religious scripture, regarded by Sikhs as their 'Eternal Guru', provides guidance on how a Sikh should live in a world whose values and ethics are changing as a result of scientific advances and changes in social organization.

Moral Living

The Gurus lived during a time when corruption and dishonesty was rife, religious worship had descended into meaningless rituals and family life had been destroyed (Banerjee 1983, McLeod 1968 and 1997). Guru Nanak spoke of an 'ideal' society, which was free of crime, dishonesty and tyranny and grounded in morality and ethical living:

> There are so many stubborn-minded intelligent people, and so many who contemplate the Vedas.
> There are so many entanglements for the soul.
> Only as *Gurmukh* do we find the Gate of Liberation.
> Truth is higher than everything; but higher still is truthful living.
> (GGS, p. 62)

I begin my analysis by briefly outlining how morality is defined from a Sikh perspective according to the Guru Granth Sahib (Singh 1996), which describes what it means to be a 'human being', and how one should live within the world, that is, the rights and duties to one's family and society as a whole:

> One who practices truth, righteous living, charity and good deeds, has the supplies for God's Path. Worldly success shall not fail him.
> (GGS, p. 743)

The following verse by Guru Nanak may be regarded as a sermon to Muslims, but encapsulates his teachings on ethical living:

> There are five prayers and five times of day for prayer; the five have five names.

Let the first be truthfulness, the second honest living, and the third
charity in the Name of God.
Let the fourth be good will to all, and the fifth the praise of the
Lord.
Repeat the prayer of good deeds, and then, you may call yourself
a Muslim.
O Nanak, the false obtain falsehood and only falsehood. (GGS,
p. 141)

Morality and ethical living therefore were viewed by the Gurus as
being dependent on human action and its consequences for all humanity. The moral individual who lives according to the teachings of God,
as set out in the Guru Granth Sahib, will serve God through the service
of others and family, there by eradicating ego and attachment to
worldly possessions and relationships. It is this attachment, which is
described as being part of *maya* (delusion), that pulls the individual
away from the one God, *Waheguru,* and prevents release from the
cycle of rebirth:

As one acts, so does he receive.
As he plants, so does he eat. (GGS, p. 662)

The individual is therefore instructed to worship and pray to
Waheguru, and remember *Waheguru* at all times if the cycle of rebirth,
death and rebirth is to be ended and, ultimately, union with God –
liberation (*mukti*) is to be achieved:

Your Name is the Fearless Lord; chanting Your Name, one does
not have to go to hell.[1] (GGS, p. 465)

Remembrance and moral behaviour is essential because God will
judge individuals on that:

The final vision of justice lies not with man
Nor any creature of the Universe;
But with God alone. (GGS, p. 144)

What one does on earth will determine what happens when one dies
and therefore performing good deeds and remembering God's name is
vital to break the cycle of reincarnation.

Guru Nanak also emphasized that true holiness and enlightenment is not achieved through renunciation of the world and becoming an ascetic or recluse. Instead, he laid out three fundamental principles to enable spiritual growth and facilitate moral and ethical living: *nam japna* (meditation on God's name), *kirat karna* (honest work) and *vand chakna* (giving to those in need). These activities, internal and external, emphasize an individual's social responsibility to the well-being of society:

Of all religions, the best religion
Is to chant the Name of the Lord and maintain pure conduct.
(GGS, p. 266)

Individual conduct therefore is very important in Sikh philosophy. True holiness and enlightenment is not achieved through denial, performing rituals or repeating God's name in a ritualistic manner. Instead, throughout the Guru Granth Sahib there is an emphasis on sincere worship, altruism and *sewa*. Guru Nanak stated that no *achar* (true moral character) can be built without the sincere worship of the *Ik Onkar* (One God) and His Name while living within this world:

The lazy unemployed has his ears pierced to look like a Yogi.
Someone else becomes a pan-handler, and loses his social status.
One who calls himself a Guru or a spiritual teacher, while he goes around begging – don't ever touch his feet.
One who works for what he eats, and gives some of what he has
– O Nanak, he knows the Path. (GGS, pp. 1245–6)

To achieve moral living and spirituality individuals have to possess and cultivate qualities such as wisdom, truthfulness, justice, temperance, courage, humility, contentment and love for humanity (Soch and Kaur 1998):

Truth and contentment govern this body-village.
Chastity, truth and self-control are in the Sanctuary of the Lord.
O Nanak, one intuitively meets the Lord, the Life of the World; the Word of the Guru's Shabad brings honour. (GGS, p. 1,037)

When these qualities are developed and cultivated, the individual recognizes that

> All virtues are Yours, Lord, I have none at all.
> Without virtue, there is no devotional worship. (GGS, p. 4)

Thus, the Gurus had recognized that the decay within society was a result of a decline in spiritual awareness. The Gurus challenged this by making the Guru Granth Sahib replete with instructions on how to achieve ultimate union with God. Many of these instructions focus on *nam japna* (meditation on God's name), *kirat karna* (honest work) and *vand chakna* (giving to those in need). For a Sikh these three principles define how to live morally and ethically in a society that is equitable and provides opportunities for all.

Haumai and the Five Vices

Although the qualities for ethical living are highlighted, the Guru Granth Sahib elucidates the difficulties that one encounters to achieve the state of *achar* – true moral living. To achieve *achar* a Sikh has to overcome *haumai* (ego – I-I). Guru Nanak, in his composition *Japji* (GGS, p. 1) identifies *haumai* as a feeling of individualism/self-centeredness, which is reinforced by five vices:

> Within this body are hidden five thieves: they are *Kam (lust or desire), krodh (anger), lobh (greed/covetousness), moh (attachment), and Ahankar (ego or pride).* They steal away the nectar within us, but we fail to realize it because of our ego and no one hears our complaint. (GGS, p. 600)

According to Guru Nanak, detachment[2] from worldly possessions is essential:

> Abandon love of family and of all affairs. Leave aside love of the world; it is a waste of time. Forsake worldly love and superstition, brother, it is all a waste of time. (GGS, p. 356)

When individuals become attached to worldly possessions, *haumai* and the accompanying five vices encourage unethical behaviour and prevent individuals from realizing God which in turn prevents release from the cycle of rebirth:

> Acting in egotism, selfishness and conceit, the foolish, ignorant, faithless cynic wastes his life. He dies in agony, like one dying of thirst; O Nanak, this is because of the deeds he has done. (GGS, p. 260)

The Gurus argued that internal actions, such as *nam simran*, are essential in the quest to overcome *haumai*:

> Remembering the True Lord in meditation, one is enlightened.
> Then, in the midst of *Maya*, he remains detached.
> Such is the Glory of the True Guru;
> in the midst of children and spouses, they attain emancipation.
> Such is the service which the Lord's servant performs,
> that he dedicates his soul to the Lord, to whom it belongs. (GGS, p. 661)

Through worship desires/vices are controlled, and if *sat* (truth) and humility (*Nimrata*) are practiced then one can become virtuous and achieve spiritual liberation because 'One who becomes *Gurmukh* knows only the One. Serving the One, peace is obtained' (GGS, p. 113), and recognizes that in the end they will have to face God on their own.

Once this has been achieved the moral person would rise above *haumai* and begin thinking about the greater good of all and how he/she can do this:

> Those who have the Treasure of the *Nam* within emancipate others as well as themselves. (GGS, p. 52)

> The *Gurmukh*, while remaining dead, is respected and approved.
> He realizes that coming and going are according to God's Will.
> He does not die, he is not reborn, and he does not suffer in pain;
> his mind merges in the Mind of God.
> Very fortunate are those who find the True Guru.
> They eradicate egotism and attachment from within.
> Their minds are immaculate, and they are never again stained with filth. They are honoured at the Door of the True Court.
> He Himself acts, and inspires all to act. (GGS, p. 1,059)

Overall, to become unattached to material and worldly possessions individuals have to live a good life, which is guided by external and internal actions. Through the internal action of *nam simran* 'lust, anger, egotism, jealousy and desires are eliminated' (GGS, p. 1,389).

These five vices and *haumai* can be controlled through the external action of *sewa*, which is essential for 'those who search for a seat in God's court' (GGS, p. 26). The concept of *sewa* makes the notion of superiority and inferiority invalid because *all* human beings are viewed as equal. This is reinforced by the Guru Granth Sahib and the *Ardas* (concluding prayer), which encourages Sikhs to be concerned with the welfare of all because of the universality of humanity.

By eradicating *haumai* and focusing on *sewa* (good actions), individuals contribute to the well-being of their community and their spiritual progression:

> O Nanak, one who earns with sweat of his brow,
> and gives some from his hands,
> He is the one who recognizes the true path. (GGS, p. 1,245)

Good actions in themselves, though, are not enough to enable one to spiritually progress; good deeds must be performed without any sense or any expectation of reward, or any sense of ego.

Sangat and Pangat

Guru Nanak founded a *Dharamsal* – a place of religious gathering where people would gather together in a congregation, called the *sadh sangat* (holy congregation) to worship and sing devotional hymns in praise of the creator. The concept and institutions of *sadh sangat*[3] and *pangat*[4] (Singh N 1990, pp. 46–50) require Sikhs to associate with saints or other religiously oriented people and collective worship is actively encouraged as a means to help the individual in *nam simran* and in overcoming worldly desires:

> The world is drunk, engrossed in sexual desire, anger and egotism. Seek the sanctuary of the saints, and fall at their feet; your suffering and darkness shall be removed. (GGS, p. 51)

In the *sangat* all Sikhs, irrespective of caste, gender or wealth, sit together, to worship and sing devotional hymns in praise of the creator, as children of the same God, and recognize that

- No one is my enemy, and I am no one's enemy. (GGS, p. 671)
- I am not called good, and I see none who are bad. (GGS, p. 1,015)
- Kabir, I am the worst of all. Everyone else is good. Whoever understands this is a friend of mine. (GGS, p. 1,364)

To conclude proceedings congregations recite a prayer called the *Ardas* – '*Sarbat the bhala*', which means '*may everyone be blessed*' or '*may good come to all*'. There is no place for dislike or hatred because all of mankind is recognized as one.

At the conclusion of proceedings, men and women, irrespective of their status, would sit together and share a meal prepared collectively by volunteers *langar*. The *langar* requires active participation from all members of the community and inculcated the essential component of *sewa,* voluntary and selfless service, carried out with humility.

Sangat and *pangat* are therefore two important institutions in Sikhism, which promote equality and *sewa* among followers. The association with holy people aids worship and concentrates the mind so that it is 'God-centred', and enables individuals to live within society ethically and morally. Such individuals become imbibed with the qualities of humility and selflessness, and work for the betterment of society.

The key qualities that individuals must accrue in order to progress spiritually are described in the above analysis. These qualities do not just benefit the individual but benefit society as a whole by making good citizens. However, for society to function equitably and justly it must also have a spiritual focus, and in Sikhism this focus is contained within two key institutions: family and marriage. I will now discuss these institutions in more detail and describe their role in the spiritual endeavour.

Marriage

In the Guru Granth Sahib, the Gurus emphasize the holy character of the family and marriage. At the time of Guru Nanak there was a belief that to achieve liberation and/or union with God, or release from the cycle of birth, death and rebirth man had to renounce his family and worldly life (*sannyas*).[5] The Gurus felt that this was destroying the institution of marriage and the moral structure of society. Guru Nanak argued that

> Without the Word of the Guru's *Shabad*, where is liberation, O mortal? Without the Lord's Name, the mortal is entangled and dies.
> Walking sticks, begging bowls, hair tufts, sacred threads, loin cloths, pilgrimages to sacred shrines and wandering all around – Without the Lord's Name, peace and tranquillity are not obtained. One who chants the Name of the Lord, Har, Har, crosses over to the other side.
> The mortal's hair may be matted and tangled upon his head, and he may smear his body with ashes; he may take off his clothes and go naked.
> But without the Lord's Name, he is not satisfied; he wears religious robes, but he is bound by the *karma* of the actions he committed in past lives. (GGS, p. 1,127)

They also felt that the practice of renunciation was promoting patriarchal oppression because it suggested that liberation was only open to men. Instead, they argued that liberation was open to all, irrespective of gender and caste:

> Men and women, throughout the four stages of life, meditate in remembrance of you. (GGS, p. 1,076)

Although open to all, liberation could only be achieved by living within society and family[6] – leading the life of a *grihasta* (householder) where everyone was equal.

> He alone is a Sannyaasi, who serves the True Guru, and removes his self-conceit from within.
> He does not ask for clothes or food; without asking, he accepts whatever he receives.
> He does not speak empty words; he gathers in the wealth of tolerance, and burns away his anger with the *Nam*.

Blessed is such a householder, Sannyaasi and Yogi, who focuses his consciousness on the Lord's feet.
Amidst hope, the Sannyaasi remains unmoved by hope; he remains lovingly focused on the One Lord.
He drinks in the sublime essence of the Lord, and so finds peace and tranquillity; in the home of his own being, he remains absorbed in the deep trance of meditation.
His mind does not waver; as *Gurmukh*, he understands. He restrains it from wandering out.
Following the Guru's Teachings, he searches the home of his body, and obtains the wealth of the *Nam*. (GGS, p. 1,013)

The Guru Granth Sahib emphasizes how family and marriage are preordained and describes how one would live within these institutions. *Grihasta* is celebrated and encouraged by the Gurus for they believed it was through the institution of marriage and family that one could develop spiritually and contribute to society as a whole. Hence, marriage and family became a holy institution and not just an organization which emerged as a result of a social contract:

Mother, father and sons are all made by the Lord;
the relationships of all are established by the Lord. (GGS, p. 494)

Thus for the Gurus marriage, monogamy[7] and family became the bedrock of society. The Gurus recognized that women are the centre of the family and not only make a valuable contribution to the development of the family, but also to the community as a whole, for it is through mothers that children are raised within the Sikh tradition.

Adultery

Monogamy and faithfulness are very important within the Sikh religious tradition because God has preordained marriage and its accompanying relationships. The ideal man and woman are devoted spouses and God-oriented. Sexual activity should only occur between husband and wife within marriage. Faithfulness is essential. A married man should consider all women, except his wife, as daughters and sisters.

One who stays away from others' wealth and others' spouses the
Lord abides near that person.
Those who do not meditate and vibrate on the Lord
I do not even want to see them. (GGS, p. 526)

However, the Gurus were aware that family values and morality
were vulnerable because people's desires, such as *kam,* can make them
engage in lust, whether in marriage or outside.

Men and women are obsessed with sex, they do not know the way
of the Lord's Name. (GGS, p. 246)

The recognition of lust and infidelity encouraged the Gurus to discuss within the Guru Granth Sahib adultery and promiscuity, and
emphasize how involvement in such activities leads individuals away
from God:

The blind fool abandons the wife of his own home,
and has an affair with another woman.
He is like the parrot, who is pleased to see the simbal tree;
but in the end, he dies, stuck to it.
The home of the sinner is on fire.
It keeps burning, and the fire cannot be extinguished.
He does not go to see where the Lord is being worshipped.
He abandons the Lord's Path, and takes the wrong path.
He forgets the Primal Lord God, and is caught in the cycle of
reincarnation. (GGS, pp. 1,163–4)

Within the *Dasam Granth* it is recorded that Guru Gobind Singh's
father Guru Tegh Bahadur told him:

O son, as long as there is life in your body, make this your sacred
duty ever to love your own wife more and more. Approach not
another woman's couch either by mistake or even in a dream.
Remember that the love of another's wife is fatal, like the blow
of a sharp dagger. Believe me; death enters the body by making
love to another's wife. They, who think it great cleverness
to enjoy another's wife, shall in the end die the death of dogs.
(*Dasam Granth*, p. 842)

From the above analysis it is clear that 'The self-willed *manmukh* is
lured by another man's wife' (GGS, p. 226), and as a consequence is

led away from their quest of liberation and become trapped in the cycle of rebirth. Guru Gobind Singh said:

> Those who indulge in illicit sexual intercourse shall be punished. (*Dasam Granth*, p. 842)

To control *kam* the Gurus advocated *nam simran*:

> Sexual desire and anger are the wounds of the soul. The evil-minded ones forget the *Nam*, and then depart. True are the teachings of the true Guru. The body and mind are cooled and soothed by the touchstone of Truth. This is the true mark of wisdom: that one remains detached, like the water-lily, or the lotus on the water. Attuned to the *Shabad*, one becomes sweet, like the juice of sugarcane. (GGS, p. 152)

Marriage and Adultery Today

Marriage, monogamy and family were promoted by the Gurus in the Guru Granth Sahib. The moral standards and expectations espoused by the Gurus have become central to Sikh culture and are binding for the community. Parents emphasize the importance of marriage, and this is further reinforced because marriage is reflected in everything from family upbringing to Bollywood movies. Women feel this pressure more than men. Single women have a 'sell by date' – after which they are not prized by society and are viewed as failures.

A fundamental, if not the most fundamental, cultural concept that ensures these religious values are adhered to today is *izzat* (honour)[8] which corresponds with one's standing within the community.

It could be argued that individuals can act otherwise, for instance, a wife can commit adultery or an unmarried girl can be sexually active and become a single mother or a married couple can divorce. However, the family and the individual will be dishonoured, shamed and ostracized.

Parents are acutely aware of the consequences of a deviation from the religious and cultural norm, and try to make their children aware of the problems that will be encountered by the individuals themselves and their family if they deviate from the norm from an early age.

Izzat, therefore, ensures that the majority of Sikh children act according to the teachings of their parents towards whom they have a moral responsibility, namely, to make it clear to relatives and friends that their parents have brought them up according to religious teachings and cultural norms (Jhutti 1998).

A successful arranged marriage for parents and the community is a symbol of status and respect, an indicator that the family has not abandoned religious and cultural values and traditions, and that they have raised and launched their children into adulthood properly, that the children respect their parents and their culture. (Ballard 1972/3 and 1982).

Although the concept of *izzat* is rooted in cultural tradition, it is quite often merged by the Sikh community into the religious tradition, as happens with other South Asian communities. It is a concept that allows Sikhs, especially men, to censure and prevent people, especially women, from doing something wrong. *Izzat* is very much defined by the male and reflects a staunchly patriarchal society. From a purely Sikh religious perspective, one may argue that if Sikhism endorses total equality between sexes then the fact that *izzat* is so weighted towards the behaviour of women fundamentally contradicts the equality principle within the Sikh religion. For example, honour is determined by the behaviour of daughters before and after marriage. By avoiding sexual relations with men before marriage, and through dressing and behaving conservatively, a woman preserves and enhances her family's honour. Conformity to marriage rules, 'tradition' and 'religious teachings' also increases and establishes one's status and *izzat* in the community.

Nowhere in the Guru Granth Sahib is divorce mentioned because marriage is preordained by God. The Gurus believed in the commitment to marriage. As a result, religion and culture dictate how Sikhs behave when a marriage breaks down. There is a strong commitment to marriage, even to a negative one, especially by women, because this was more acceptable than being divorced. The consequences of marital breakdown are deeply ingrained in the minds of men and women, but especially women. For example, women are conscious of the fact that if they were to separate from their partner, speculations immediately begin as to why the marriage broke down. Culturally, the failure of a marriage is always assumed to be the woman's fault, and is a blemish on her reputation, and her parents are criticized for not bringing up their daughter properly. Thus, divorce, adultery and sexual promiscuity not only result in disgrace for the woman concerned, but for her family too, because the chances for younger brothers and sisters, even cousins, making a 'decent' marriage are believed to be spoiled (Jhutti 1998).

However, in contemporary Sikh society, divorce, as a result of adultery and sexual promiscuity, is on the rise. In the past, Sikh divorce figures, if there were any, would have been low, but that was because many people were locked in unhappy marriages due to religious and cultural influences. Today, women are financially independent, and while keeping up a respectable appearance for the community is still important, some men and women no longer feel it outweighs personal happiness.

In one interview a young lady told me:

> For Sikhs, marriage and the commitment to it is very important. It is a religious commitment, which you make in front of your Guru and family. This and *izzat* means that you have to work hard to ensure that your marriage does not breakdown. However, the younger generation don't seem to be taking this that seriously because divorce in our community is on the rise. You can tell this from the matrimonial column and internet sites.

From talking to young Sikhs it was clear that immediate individual fulfilment is what matters. In the past, marriage meant individuals were committed and would endure difficulties. However, this is no longer the case. Among some Sikhs there is a 'me-first' culture, which has resulted in divorce becoming an acceptable option even in trivial situations, such as living with the extended family. For example, one young girl told me:

> My situation was hard because I was living with my in-laws, and that wasn't what I wanted from a marriage, and I decided I wasn't going to put up with it when my husband didn't listen to me.

Thus, the sancity of marriage is being questioned, and many sikhs, especially the elders, would argue that Western culture and education is contributing to the rise in divorce, remarriage and single parenthood.

Inter-caste and Interfaith Marriages

In recent years there has been a growing trend of inter-caste marriage and interfaith marriages. Both forms of marriages are discouraged by the Sikh religious hierarchy and Sikh families.

Interfaith marriages: The Sikh religious community fears that inter-faith marriages will eventually lead to the disintegration of the religion, given the relatively small numbers of Sikhs in the world (this is a similar problem to that faced by the Jewish community around interfaith marriage issues). In May 2007, the religious community in India, including the SGPC President, Avtar Singh Makkar, agreed to ban interreligious marriages in gurdwaras.[9] In response, the *Akal Takht* – the Supreme seat of authority of the Sikhs – issued a *Hukumnama* (decree) regarding this matter on 16 August 2007 stating that the Sikh marriage ceremony should only be conducted when both bride and groom are Sikhs (as a respect towards the religion). If the couple or either one of them is not a Sikh, then they must embrace the Sikh faith. This includes that they must change their last name to 'Singh' or 'Kaur' officially before the Marriage Ceremony.

Inter-caste marriages: Caste affiliation and identity is still firmly rooted within the Sikh community. Sikh families, including baptized Sikhs, still continue the tradition of marrying within the same caste. Marrying outside one's caste is still taboo, particularly for the so-called higher caste groups among Sikhs such as the jats.

Over the last decade or so there has been an increase in inter-caste marriages. Couples who do marry outside their caste base their argument on the teachings of the Gurus: that there is no such thing as caste. These marriages, although defined as 'love marriages', are organized and disguised by parents as arranged marriages in an attempt to maintain their honour.

Thus, conforming to the ideal that is espoused by the Gurus is important because it demonstrates an acceptance of the religious teachings. Culturally, marriage to a Sikh partner is essential and necessary for men and women, but especially for women. For women it is a passport into the mainstream of life, and even a negative relationship is more acceptable than none. Nevertheless, it is clear that things are changing due to westernization. For example, an increase in divorce and inter-caste marriages.

Marriage = Family?

While marriage is itself important for the structure of society, so is the purpose of marriage. The Gurus made marriage and conception a sacred act, which was inseparable:

> Through the union of mother and father, the foetus is formed. The egg and sperm join together to make the body. (GGS, p. 1,013)

Sikh theology, like Catholic theology (Russell 1996) supports the idea that there is only one kind of morally good sexual act: sex between a man and a woman who are married and who are having sex to conceive and raise children to perpetuate God's creation.

Since the purpose of marriage is to have children so that God's creation can be perpetuated, the issue of family planning and contraception raises problems. Sikh teachings on birth control are often based on Sikh interpretations of the meaning of marriage, sex and the family as contained in the Guru Granth Sahib. Until the development of contraception, Sikhs have used self-control to regulate sexual activities in harmony with nature, for instance, abstention (not having sex) or using a woman's menstrual cycle to inform the couple of a woman's fertile time. With the recent development of various forms of contraception,[10] Sikhs have had to address the question of whether contraception can be used. There are no injunctions in Sikhism against the use of contraceptives within a married relationship and no insistence on abstinence in the Guru Granth Sahib (Gatrad 2005, p. 354). The answer to this question is derived from an interpretation of teachings rather than from strict statements in the Guru Granth Sahib.

Conservative and religious Sikhs would advocate that if one were to follow the teachings in the Guru Granth Sahib, then natural methods of contraception such as controlling ones sexual desires are preferred to artificial methods and devices. This is because the Pill or the so-called morning-after pill goes against natural law and gives human beings the power to decide when a new life should begin, when actually that power belongs to God. Additionally, they would argue that contraception is anti-life and is a form of abortion, especially the morning-after pill. However, it could also be argued that natural methods of contraception also do this.

Within marriage the argument against contraception is that it encourages extramarital affairs, but most importantly it stops couples from fulfilling their duty, namely, having children. Nevertheless, whatever the reason against contraception within marriage, it is clear from current research that within the Sikh community it is felt that the decision of family planning to regulate the size and spacing of their family should be left to the married couple.

Contraception and Sex Education

The Sikh religious community believes, like many other religious communities, that the responsibility of telling children about sex and relationships lies with the parents and not someone else, namely, teachers. The problem with this is that most Sikh parents would probably be too embarrassed to talk about sex with their children, and so sex education classes at school may be the only place where Sikh youngsters talk openly about these issues with adults.

The consensus of the community, after having spoken to religious leaders, was that teaching sex education in schools could have unintentional consequences. One member of the religious community in the United Kingdom, and a father of three teenage daughters said:

> Contraception and sex education in schools promotes youngsters to do wrong things and to become promiscuous. It does not promote proper values that I would want my children to receive and having sex outside of marriage is ok.

From this comment it is evident that, while sex education in schools is thought to be wrong, so is the availability of contraception to young children. The belief is that contraception, such as the pill, the morning-after pill (referred to as 'emergency contraception') or condoms, is wrong because it encourages youngsters to indulge in sexual activities. It is evident that Sikhs believe that contraception and sex education for the young goes against religious teachings and weakens morality, the sanctity of marriage and the status of the family.

Abortion

When we discuss contraception, particularly the morning-after pill, another controversial issue is raised – abortion. The Guru Granth Sahib does not deal with abortion (or indeed any bioethical issues). There is not a single statement in the Guru Granth Sahib which could be interpreted to allow abortion. As a result, abortion presents a moral dilemma for Sikhs, because it is not clear in what circumstances it would be permissible.

According to the Guru Granth Sahib human life begins immediately at the moment of conception and that creation of life is the will of God. Conception signifies an event in which God has created a vessel for the soul to reside and develop, but most importantly for God to be present in:

> From the union of the mother's egg and the father's sperm, the form of infinite beauty has been created.
> The blessings of light all come from You; You are the Creator Lord, pervading everywhere. (GGS, p. 1,022)

The embryo or zygote that is created upon conception is a divine gift, which has to be nurtured and nourished to prepare it for the world, and the time in the womb is a valuable element of the spiritual development of the human being.[11] This is in opposition to medical research which guided the UK Parliamentary Science and Technology Committee in 2007. The research suggested that a foetus does not have any feelings before 24 weeks and is not viable if born that early (the UK Parliamentary Science and Technology Committee STC 2007, pp. 13–25).

For Sikhs an embryo or foetus has feelings as soon as conception takes place. For example, in the Guru Granth Sahib there are verses which describe how the unborn child has the ability to meditate upon God's name as soon as it is conceived, and although the womb is viewed as a dismal, frightening and even a fiery place, God is seen as providing nourishment and protection for the unborn child:

> In the first watch of the night, O my merchant friend, you were cast into the womb, by the Lord's Command.
> Upside-down, within the womb, you performed penance, O my

merchant friend, and you prayed to your Lord and Master.
You uttered prayers to your Lord and Master, while upside-down,
and you meditated on Him with deep love and affection.
You came into this Dark Age of Kali Yuga naked, and you shall
depart again naked.
As God's Pen has written on your forehead, so it shall be with
your soul.
Says Nanak, in the first watch of the night, by the *Hukam* of the
Lord's Command, you enter into the womb. (GGS, p. 74)

Sikh Practice Today Regarding Abortion

Since Sikh theology argues that the soul is 'born' immediately upon
conception it can be inferred that it would be a sin to abort a foetus
because, first, it is a human life created by God, and second, to abort
this life would interfere in the creative work of God. Despite this clear
theological viewpoint of when life is created, abortion is not uncom-
mon among the Sikh community in India and the diaspora. Abortion
is not due to unintended pregnancies from extramarital affairs or sexual relationships outside of marriage. This has been limited or prevented by notions of honour and shame (*izzat*). Instead, abortion is
prevalent within marriage due to the advent of foetal sonograms/ultra-
sounds, which allow couples to identify the sex of the foetus. Once the
sex has been identified, many couples will abort the foetus if they are
informed that it is a female, due to the cultural preference for sons, a
preference which is influenced by social and economic factors (see
Chapter 3 for more discussion). In these circumstances the termination
is not referred to as abortion, but as female foeticide. Within India and
Punjab this problem is widespread. Members of the Sikh community
engage in the practices of female foetal abortion and gender pre-
selection (see Chapter 3 for more discussion). However, it is also growing among the Sikhs in the diaspora.

Sex Determination – A Boy or a Girl –
Who Should Decide?

From the above it is clear that abortion is gaining prominence among
Sikh couples after they have ascertained the sex of the foetus and this
goes against Sikh religious teachings, because the sex of a child is

preordained and God's *hukam* (will). Children are 'gifts' from God and couples should accept God's will (Gatrad 2005, p. 354).

Medical advances in procedures that allow couples to determine the sex of a child before it has been conceived are also a challenge to the Sikh community because they also interfere with God's will (*hukam*) and the natural process. For example, Preimplantation Genetic Diagnosis (PGD) – the creation of embryos outside the body – which allows the parents to choose a male or female embryo for implantation (Handyside et al. 1997, Robertson 2003, Sermon et al. 2004), or sperm sorting, which involves dividing a sperm sample into 'male' and 'female' groups, are being used by members of the Sikh community to determine the sex of a child.

In the United Kingdom, gender selection is not allowed under the law; however, in India it is fair to say that sex selection is available on demand. Sikh couples from the United Kingdom have been known to go to India for PGD treatment, or even for scans to find out the sex of a child. In Punjab there are many clinics that will offer such services. Sikhs are using these clinics to ensure the birth of a male child because, like most South Asian cultures, a son is valued more than a daughter because a son will contribute economically to the family and ensure continuation of the family line.[12]

While most couples would use such treatment to guarantee the birth of a son, there are other couples who may use it to balance their family. For example, where a family already has three boys they may use PGD to guarantee the birth of a girl. This is not that common, though. In such circumstances it could be argued that if the couple was living according to the teachings then they would recognize that it may be their *karma* just to have boys.

It is important to note from the above discussion that although scientific and technological innovations were intended to improve people's quality of life, these innovations, such as ultrasounds and sonograms, have been abused for cultural reasons, namely, the preference for sons.

Problematic Pregnancy

If aborting a pregnancy that is a result of extramarital relations or on the grounds of the gender of the foetus is morally wrong according to Sikh teachings, how is an abortion viewed when the pregnancy is problematic or because it is the result of rape?

As there is no specific dictate in religious texts about abortions most Sikhs would argue that in such circumstances, the right response would be one of compassion for the mother and the child. For example, if there were circumstances where the mother's life was threatened by the continuation of the pregnancy, then termination could be acceptable, but this would all be dependent on the circumstances involved.

A hospital chaplain in his late sixties emphasized this point:

> All human life is of equal value. If a mother had cancer one cannot say whether the life of the child in the womb is more or less important than that of the mother. You have to be aware of all the reasons for why a couple might abort a foetus. For example, if a mother is ill with cancer and the only way to treat her is for her to abort her child and have chemotherapy, and she already has two young children then there can be no moral objections. Here the mother, even if her action leads to the death of her unborn child is making sure that her living children have a mother.

Currently, an expectant mother faced with the news that her child may be disabled is likely to be guided towards aborting the foetus by her medical doctors.[13] In such a situation where the child could have a congenital disease or abnormality, some Sikhs would argue that the decision is the woman's, and that she should be allowed to decide along the lines of whether she could raise and care for a child with an abnormality. The counter argument against free will and choice involves the notion of God's *hukam* (will). It could be argued that if the teachings of the Guru Granth Sahib are to be adhered to, then one has to go through such a pregnancy because it was God's will and was a result of one's *karma*.

Whatever the circumstances, it is clear that there is nothing in the Guru Granth Sahib about abortion. The teachings on birth, family and so on can be interpreted and consulted for guidance in difficult situations such as rape and pregnancy. Sikhs will interpret certain parts of the text individually and make a personal decision accordingly, which would be dependent on a number of factors. It is because of differences in circumstances that there are a variety of interpretations of what can and cannot be done.

Homosexuality and Same-Sex Marriages

In the last two decades, Sikhs have been confronted by the issue of homosexuality and same-sex marriage. The question is how should Sikhs interpret and deal with such modern issues because religious teachings as contained in the Guru Granth Sahib do not refer to homosexuality as the Abrahamic traditions do. Instead, in the Guru Granth Sahib only marriage between a man and a woman is openly described and discussed. The Gurus argued that liberation and salvation was available for everyone through *grishti* (householder life), which was essential for having and raising children who were necessary for the continuation of God's creation.

The Gurus' silence on homosexuality has led to ambivalence on the topic. To answer whether homosexuality and same-sex marriages are permitted, Sikhs are either reinterpreting the text for themselves or are turning to religious authorities in India (SGPC and *Akal Takht*) for answers. However, the variety of responses has created tension.

The issue of homosexuality became a public issue for the Sikhs in 2005 when the highest Sikh religious authority was asked by Sikh Canadian MPs who had to vote on the Gay Marriage Bill (Bill C38: The Civil Marriage Act) what the Sikh perspective was on this issue. In its response, the *Akal Takht*[14] (Seat of the Immortal One) described homosexuality as 'against the Sikh religion and the Sikh code of conduct and totally against the laws of nature'. It called on the Sikh MPs not to support laws which permitted same-sex marriage in Canada,[15] because civil partnerships/marriages are not equivalent to marriage between man and woman because such a partnership cannot fulfil the function of having children.

Giani (priest) Joginder Singh Vedanti said:

The basic duty of Sikh MPs in Canada should be to support laws that stop this kind of practice homosexuality, because there are thousands of Sikhs living in Canada, to ensure that Sikhs do not fall prey to this practice. Speaking to the Canadian Sikh MPs who had to vote on the Bill he said: 'The Sikh religion would never accept such MPs. Nobody would support such a person having such dirty thoughts in their mind because it is against the

Sikh religion and the Sikh code of conduct and totally against the laws of nature. Sikhs around the world must maintain fidelity to these religious teachings,' he argued, 'and no politician is exempt'.

Giani Vedanti's words were echoed by Manjit Singh Kalkatta, another highly respected Sikh preacher who sits on the governing body of the Harmandar Sahib, the Shiromani Gurdwara Prabandhak Committee (SGPC). 'The advice given by the highest Sikh temporal authority to every Sikh is that it is unnatural and ungodly and the Sikh religion cannot support it'.

From the above instructions it becomes clear that homosexuality has been stigmatized because the religious community perceived a conflict between religion and sexual orientation. One priest from the United Kingdom said:

A marriage cannot happen unless it involves the opposite sex. Two men or two women cannot marry. If they do, then that marriage cannot be classified as a marriage because marriage is an institution created for the production of children. Same sex couples cannot do this. Therefore Sikhs cannot do this.

A new priest from India commented that

People of the same sex cannot enter into marriage. It is not possible. The thing that people of the same sex are entering into is not real or legal in God's eyes. You may do everything to make it look like the real thing, but God and we all know it is not.

He went on to comment how:

A union that has been was instituted by God has been reduced by humans to mean nothing at all.

Conservative Sikhs therefore believe that because the Guru Granth Sahib is the complete guide to life, and because there is no mention of marriage or a relationship between individuals of the same sex, it is against God's will and against 'natural law' since procreation cannot happen. The belief that it is 'unnatural', against nature and endangers the moral well-being of Sikh society means that it is discouraged and actively forbidden.

The fear of stigmatization and ostracization has meant that Sikhs do not 'come out', but instead marry and have children to maintain their family honour. To find an openly gay Sikh man or lesbian woman is difficult. Most keep their sexual orientation hidden as they are aware of the consequences.

Liberal Views on Homosexuality and Same-Sex Marriages

We have to draw attention to the thoughts of liberal Sikhs who offer a different view, which is often overlooked and delegitimized in favour of the view held by conservative Sikhs.[16] During the course of this research I spoke to some liberal Sikhs, some of whom were gay and baptized, and these interviews elicited some interesting feedback regarding homosexuality and same-sex marriages.

Liberal Sikhs believe that teachings should be reinterpreted in light of new modern-day issues, such as homosexuality so that Sikhs who find themselves in such situations do not have to abandon their religion due to prejudice and stigmatization. The argument that they posit is that, Guru Nanak's emphasis on universal equality and brotherhood is applicable to all, including homosexuals. Some of the verses that were quoted included:

God is our Father; we all are His children, hence equal. No one of us by birth is superior or inferior to others. (GGS, p. 97)

There is only one breath; all are made of the same clay; the light within all is the same.
The One Light pervades all the many and various beings. This Light intermingles with them, but it is not diluted or obscured. (GGS, p. 96)

He is within – see Him outside as well; there is no one, other than Him. As *Gurmukh*, look upon all with the single eye of equality; in each and every heart, the Divine Light is contained. (GGS, p. 599)

Liberal Sikhs therefore argue that homosexuality is normal for a minority of adults, and that they should not be ostracized from society because in the eyes of the Gurus, all are created equally.

Regarding the modern-day issue of same-sex marriages, liberal Sikhs argue that, since it is not discussed in the Guru Granth Sahib, then the family lifestyle that the Gurus encourage can be cultivated by two members of the same sex. Some liberal Sikhs have reinterpreted the *Lavan*[17] (Appendix) very liberally. Through their reinterpretation they argue that since the four verses are non-gender specific, then same-sex marriages are possible because the use of gender is metaphorical: to show how the bride (devotee) becomes devoted to her husband (God) and attains enlightenment. However, conservative Sikhs dismiss this argument. They argue that since man and woman are only mentioned in a relationship that emphasizes the relationship between the soul and God, in no way does it suggest that same-sex marriages are permissible.

What Is Happening Today?

It is clear that although liberal Sikhs are engaging with the debate, conservative Sikhs are not. Instead, they are relying on a traditional reading of the Guru Granth Sahib to reinforce the notion of family – one man, one woman and children – as the norm. Most Sikhs therefore take a conservative line and there appears to be no room for variance, and any liberal views are condemned, although they do exist. This religiously conservative view is also reinforced by Sikh culture. From a cultural perspective, the kinship system, which continues to underlie the entire Sikh social organization, plays an important role in ensuring that children and parents adhere to religious teachings and cultural traditions. Hence, family and the community are the principal influencers when educating and determining an individual's basic roles and behaviour with reference to homosexuality. Sikhs are aware that by accepting liberal views or by behaving in a 'modern' or 'progressive' way, such as adopting Western social and cultural conventions, they will be seen to be un-Sikh.

As a result of the negative religious and cultural perceptions of same-sex relationships, Sikhs who are gay or lesbian do not 'come out', but keep that identity hidden. For example gay men and lesbian women are turning to each other through social networking and matrimonial sites to arrange marriages of convenience, while maintaining their own homosexual relationships.[18] They are leading double lives so that they maintain not only their family's honour, but also ensure that they are not ostracized.[19] As a result, gay people are invisible, and this has led to a false belief among many Sikhs that homosexuality does not exist in the Sikh community. This is similar to views about the existence of divorce in the past. Due to honour, divorce used to be avoided: couples used to resolve their problems within the framework of the marriage, for instance they would remain married but lead separate lives, and this led to the false belief that there were no broken marriages (Jhutti 1998).

In spite of certain alternate modern and liberal views, the strong conservative ideas on morality with reference to homosexuality have made Sikhs intensely loyal to the religious teachings of the Guru Granth Sahib, especially those concerning marriage and family. As a result, no attempt has been made to accommodate gay or lesbian sikhs, only a complete rejection of their existence.

Organ Donation and Transplantation

Through medical advances new forms of treatment have been developed which rely on people donating their organs, such as kidneys, eyes and heart to others when they die, or in certain circumstances while they are still alive. However, Sikhs worldwide have not shown a willingness to take part in organ donation, and this is confirmed by interviews with respondents, most of whom did not carry an organ donation card. Why this is the case is difficult to ascertain. Respondents, whatever their age, could not give a reason for why they did not want their organs to be donated, even though all acknowledged that they may one day need an organ.

The religious teachings within the Guru Granth Sahib can be interpreted to suggest that there is no prohibition on the issue of organ donation and organ transplantation. This is for two reasons. First, organ donation is permissible because Sikh theology and philosophy places great emphasis on *sewa* and altruism: acts performed without the expectation of rewards or personal benefit. Second, Sikhs fundamentally believe that the body, along with its constituent parts, is just clothing for the soul and is discarded at death. The organs are therefore viewed as the machinery, which allows the physical body to function, but unlike the soul they perish once death occurs, while the soul moves on to its next journey.[20]

The soul, a divine spark, is either taken back to join *Waheguru* when a person is finally released from the cycle of rebirth or is reborn.[21] Therefore, for Sikhs, death is not the end, but it is the soul that imbues the body with the life force and which is indestructible. Death merely marks the release of the 'knot' between body and soul:

> Their fears and doubts are dispelled, the knot of death is untied, and they never have to walk on Death's path. (GGS, p. 691)

There appears to be no straightforward religious explanation for why Sikhs do not practice organ donation when they are alive or dead. The reasons may be less to do with religion and more to do with misconceptions about organ donation, such as the belief that doctors may not try as hard to save somebody who has agreed to organ donation after death, or it may be due to a fear that if they donate while alive, they may be disfigured, or the fear that they may fall ill and need the organ they have donated, for example, a kidney.

Death – Whose Command?

Assisted Suicide/Euthanasia and Mercy Killings

There has been a lot of debate around the issue of living wills, assisted suicide/euthansia and mercy killings in the last two decades in the United Kingdom , particularly from a Christian perspective. Sikhs have not addressed this issue. To answer whether a Sikh can take someone's life out of compassion and as an act of mercy one needs to consider how the Gurus viewed life. From an analysis of the Guru Granth Sahib it is clear that the Gurus had a high respect for life, which they viewed as a gift from God. Thus, a Sikh has to accept that the life he/she has was decided by our *karma* and that God has determined how many 'breaths' we breathe.

The injunction that God has preordained how long we live and whether we have to suffer goes against the increasing modern practice of living wills, euthanasia or mercy killing. As a result, there is no place for mercy killing, assisted suicide or euthanasia in Sikhism for death happens when God commands it:

> The Righteous Judge of Dharma is relentless; he counts each and every breath. (GGS, p. 1,354)

The Gurus also argued that suffering is a part of the human condition and has a place in God's scheme. Suffering also prompts man to turn his thoughts to God:

Suffering is the medicine, and pleasure the disease, because where there is pleasure, there is no desire for God. (GGS, p. 469)

Hence, individuals should have the moral courage to bear suffering and this is achieved through prayer. For example, in the first line of Sukhmani Sahib, Guru Arjan tells us,

To the one who meditates on Him, there comes a perfect peace.
And all pain and sorrows depart.
Meditate on Him, who contains the universe.
Whose Holy *Nam* is the whisper on the lips of the entire creation.
(GGS, p. 262)

The Sikh Gurus believed that suffering was part of the operation of *karma*, and human beings should not only accept it without complaint but also act so as to make the best of the situation that has been given to them. Individuals should live and suffer the tests that God has put in their life and demonstrate an acceptance of God's *hukam* to demonstrate their faith and trust in God. In such situations it is not just the *karma* of the sufferer that is affected but also that of his/ her carers. Looking after a terminally ill individual may be seen as a test for the carer(s), which he/she must bear in order to progress spiritually.

Living Wills
Since God has given life and since Sikhs are supposed to live according to the will of God, no one has the right to decide when life should conclude; that is a decision for God. If such a request is made in a 'living will' it could be argued that Sikhs should not follow through on such a request because to do so would mean crossing a moral boundary and taking a life before God's command. Living wills, like assisted suicide, will prevent an individual's spiritual progression towards liberation from the cycle of rebirth and union with God.

Although the above does sound absolute, it is clear that because God has given individuals free will then what Sikhs will do when confronted by a particular situation, such as a coma (thereby given a choice to end life) or cancer (being offered a treatment to prolong a terminal state) may be dependent on their circumstances, and their reading and interpretation of the Guru Granth Sahib.

Although some Sikhs might argue that such intervention is okay because a 'just' God would not want his children to suffer, most Sikhs would believe suffering is due to past *karma*, and that the timing of birth and death is God's prerogative and under His command and should be left in His hands. Such conformity demonstrates that many Sikhs, young and old, aware of the theory of reincarnation, believe that to take one's life through suicide to avoid suffering would make them go against God's will and that they would be punished through the cycle of rebirth. Thus, a natural death is the only option because it guarantees a return to the source: God.

Conclusion

In conclusion the Guru Granth Sahib is grounded in a historical context which was influenced by socio-economic and political circumstances. The focus on moral and ethical issues emphasizes, particularly within the realm of family, how the Gurus were concerned with society and human action. These same issues of family, marriage and how to be a good individual exist today, but they are complicated by social and scientific advances, which have led to issues such as abortion, homosexuality, divorce, adultery, single parenthood, the breakdown of the extended family, and euthanasia, all of which challenge the Sikh ethos. On the surface, these matters go against Sikh religious and cultural teachings, and it is for this reason that a community which deeply values its religious traditions, social norms and customs needs to address how to perceive morality and ethics with reference to modern-day issues and how to understand them from a religious perspective.

This chapter demonstrates that spirituality provides the foundations and principles for moral and ethical living for Sikhs. The religious, but also cultural goal for a Sikh is to lead a 'good life', which is achieved by following the moral and ethical values as put forward by the Gurus in the Guru Granth Sahib. For example, Guru Nanak, a firm believer in the duties of an individual to family and society, advocated that a moral society could be achieved through ethical values such as integrity, responsibility and fairness, but most importantly that these had to be practiced through *nam japana* (meditation on God's name), *kirat karna* (honest work) and *vand chakna* (giving to those in need). These activities should ideally be done within a family and community structure.

These core values continue to be adhered to today because what is contained in the Guru Granth Sahib is viewed as 'law'. Most Sikhs live according to the values and morals advocated in the Guru Granth Sahib so that they behave in an ethical and responsible manner, which would be acceptable to God, since to do otherwise would hinder spiritual progression.

Using the Guru Granth Sahib to address contemporary issues is problematic, as with any other religious text, because it reinforces ethics and values of a different era. The Guru Granth Sahib could be seen to be presenting a picture of a fixed and unchanging tradition, which does not attempt to address changing needs and circumstances, for example, homosexuality and organ donation. This is not the case though. This ignores how Sikhs, who are firmly located within their religion, are deciphering, interpreting and reinterpreting the Guru Granth Sahib, without changing the core teachings to make their way through contemporary society according to God's will.

Through this process of interpretation and reinterpretation, it is clear that in certain situations there may be several right answers, and that this would be dependent on interpretation, which in turn is dependent on a number of factors, such as circumstance, gender, age and education. However, no matter what the interpretation, it is clear that all Sikhs want to do the 'right' thing.

Where there is a variation in meaning and understanding, the core and fundamental concepts of the faith are not generally criticized or dismissed. Also, modernity has not meant that religious beliefs are disregarded. For example, if we consider contraception, it is clear that up until the 1960s it was relatively unusual for a Sikh couple to remain childless out of choice or delay having a child. However, the introduction of the contraceptive pill has given married women freedom and control over when to have children. Having children is no longer an automatic priority, and as a result an increasing number of Sikh women are putting off having their first child until their late thirties or early forties. Delaying having children may not go against the teachings because the intention is still to have children; however, some Sikhs may view the use of contraception as unethical since God's *hukam* is being interfered with. It could also be argued that while

Sikhism promotes the value of life, certain forms of contraception, especially the morning-after pill, go against the pro-life ethos of the Sikh religion.

Thus, modern issues need to be challenged and addressed by Sikh scholars and religious authorities through a critical engagement with the Guru Granth Sahib. They will have to critique and interpret the teachings in light of modern-day issues, to provide guidance on what ethical issues such as abortion, contraception and euthanasia mean for Sikhs. This is being done to some extent, but, as in any other religious community, schisms and tensions are appearing once decisions are made – especially those that are made mandatory. Compliance is not always guaranteed. For example, from past history it is clear that not all Sikhs will comply with religious dictates. In 1998 the Jathedar of the *Akal Takht* passed a *hukamnama* (edict). The edict said that all Sikhs had to sit on the floor when eating *langar*. Some gurdwaras have endorsed this in the United Kingdom, but others have not. Decisions about whether to comply or not have been influenced by the makeup of the managing committee of the gurdwara, pressure from the *sangat* or recognition that nowhere is it written in the Guru Granth Sahib that you cannot sit and eat *langar* at a table.

This may seem a trivial example, but it highlights that there are varied responses to dictates, which range from ambivalence to endorsement to denunciation. However, what is clear is that dictates relating to moral and ethical issues such as marriage will always be complied with by most Sikhs. Marriage has remained an important religious and social marker in an individual's life, and it has been preserved without a departure from the way it is described within the Guru Granth Sahib. As a result, the 2005 dictate about same-sex marriages has been adhered to because any move away from marriage between a man and a woman is viewed as an attack on morality and a deviation from the religious teachings contained within the Guru Granth Sahib. Hence, compliance is essential. If this dictate is not followed or adhered to, the religious community and the Sikh community as a whole have the moral voice and ability to enforce what they believe to be appropriate behaviour through notions of *izzat* and shame. As a result, there is a broad and genuine adherence to moral and ethical values which have been stressed within the Guru Granth Sahib.

Overall, it is clear that the Guru Granth Sahib and the Sikh religion have not declined as a guiding moral force. Instead, we are seeing diversity among the Sikh community with regard to interpretation and reinterpretation of certain values that are advocated in the Guru Granth Sahib. Morals and ethical values, which are in opposition to current issues, are slowly being engaged with to allow the religion to evolve, survive and prosper within the modern world.

Chapter 5

Identity – Who Is a Sikh . . . Continued?

Introduction

This chapter will examine the debate surrounding the question of 'Who Is a Sikh?' This has been an ongoing debate with definitions being drawn up in the various Gurdwara Acts and *Rehats*, especially the 1950 *Rehat Maryada*. The question of identity has come to the forefront recently with legal cases in India and the diaspora attempting to define who is a Sikh. The leading debate in the British courts has centred on the issue of whether being Sikh is hereditary or a matter of 'appropriate' belief and behaviour (Nesbitt 2000, Sidhu 1993, Singh and Tatla 2006, Tatla 2001). While in Punjab, India, the law defines Sikh identity as being dependent on behaviour and having taken baptism (*amrit*).

It is extremely difficult to find a fully clarified and accepted definition for the question of who is a Sikh. There is much discussion and discord on the issue, mainly centring on the issue of the status of *Khalsa* (*Amritdhari*) Sikhs versus non-*Khalsa* Sikhs. There are generally three main types of Sikhs: *amritdhari, keshdhari* and *sehajdhari* (McLeod 1989b). A further minor category includes convert Sikhs, referred to as *Gora* Sikhs. This chapter will address how these categories have an impact on the question of Sikh identity.

To answer the question of 'Who is a Sikh?', the historical development of Sikh identity, starting with the Sikh Gurus, will be considered first. This section will focus on how the Gurus defined identity. For example, Sikhs at the time of Guru Nanak were referred to as Nanak Panthis – and this definition did not refer to an external identity, but defined Sikh identity on the basis of practice and belief of Guru

Nanak's teachings. This changed at the time of the sixth Guru, Guru Hargobind, who introduced the concept of *miri/piri* – spiritual (*miri*) and temporal (*piri*) authority, respectively. Finally, an external identity was given by Guru Gobind Singh through the *Khalsa* (pure brotherhood).

After the death of Guru Gobind Singh, Sikh identity was in flux for approximately 200 years, due to the social and cultural environment in India. During this period there were two types of Sikhs: *amritdhari* (baptized) and *sehajdhari* Sikhs (defined as 'slow adopters' of the faith). Although there were two types of Sikhs, it was evident that Sikhs did not look much different from the Hindus because they were practising, and using Hindu customs in their religious practices and day-to-day lives. As a result, towards the end of the eighteenth century and the beginning of the nineteenth century, some Sikhs made a concerted effort to reintroduce a Sikh identity which was defined by the teachings of the Gurus, in particular Guru Gobind Singh. Since the nineteenth century, identity was defined by legislation in Punjab, India, for example, the *Singh Sabha* Movement (1873) and the Gurdwara Acts in India, Punjab (1919, 1925 and 1971) and finally within the *Rehat Maryada*, the Sikh Code of Conduct. Identity will be discussed with reference to these legislations.

Identity will also be considered with reference to three legal cases (one from Punjab and two from the United Kingdom), comparing and contrasting how they define a Sikh. The analysis will demonstrate how the theological definition of a Sikh espoused by the Indian courts is not sufficient and does not reflect the diversity within the Sikh faith. Finally, Sikh identity in the diaspora will be discussed, especially the disillusionment among young Sikhs.

The Historical Development of Sikh Identity under the Gurus

During the formative years of the religion the definition of a 'true Sikh' was very wide and did not follow the structured definitions we see today.

McLeod placed Guru Nanak's teachings firmly in the North Indian Sant tradition, at least in terms of antecedents and influence. McLeod points to the uniquely clear and integrated message of Guru Nanak, which, while different from this tradition, also shared many similarities, such as a doctrine of deliverance where caste played no role.

Grewal, on the other hand, focuses more on Guru Nanak's rejection of contemporary religious beliefs and practices. He 'highlights the distinctive quality of Guru Nanak's message in the context of his times as well as the originality of his response' (Singh and Barrier 1999, p. 71).

Cole and Sambhi (1993 and 1985, pp. 7–38) also point to the fact that Guru Nanak set his teachings aside from those of the earlier Indian teachers by rejecting the conventions of his time. For example, for Guru Nanak salvation and spiritual liberation were achieved by rejecting renunciation and living the life of a householder (*grishti*).

Early Sikhs began to use hymns in congregational worship, a sign that under Guru Nanak the foundations of a community with its own separate identity was beginning to form. This identity was further strengthened by Nanak's successor, Guru Angad, who formulated the Gurmukhi script and established a center for the community based around *langar* (free kitchen) to erode caste inequality.

Guru Amar Das, the third Guru, developed an administrative system within the community, as well as introducing distinctive birth and death ceremonies. He also contributed sacred verses, including those used in the Sikh marriage ceremony. Guru Ram Das founded a new city, called Amritsar, where Guru Arjan Dev built the *Harmandar Sahib* (Golden Temple). Guru Arjan also compiled the first canon of scripture, the *Adi Granth*, which contained the works of the first five Gurus. It was from this time that the status of Guru began to be imbued with attributes of royalty, and the title 'True King' was being applied both to God and the Gurus (Singh and Barrier 1999, p. 80). Guru Hargobind introduced the martial elements to the identity. He wore two swords, representing his spiritual (*miri*) and temporal (*piri*) authority respectively, and built the *Akal Takht*, one of five 'Seats of Power' of the Sikhs. This, with the martyrdom of Guru Tegh Bahadur, the ninth Guru, for his commitment to religious freedom developed an identity that was based on the concept of 'soldier saint': spiritually pure people who uphold the principles of equality, justice and compassion by force when necessary.

It is this duality of a temporal and spiritual person that found its ultimate expression under the tenth Guru, Gobind Singh. In 1699 Guru Gobind Singh took the actions of Guru Hargobind one step further. While Guru Hargobind had added a militant aspect to the religion, Guru Gobind Singh formalized this idea and created a specific group, the *Khalsa* that, among other things,[1] was meant to protect

the Sikh faith and its people. This was done in response to the contin-
ued persecution of Sikhs under the Mughal Empire. The Sikhs had
attempted, through peaceful means, to coexist with the Mughals, but
this proved unsuccessful. The death of Guru Tegh Bahadur is regarded
as the catalyst that sparked Guru Gobind Singh into formalizing this
military order. He is quoted as saying, 'When all avenues have been
explored, all means tried, it is rightful to draw the sword out of the
scabbard and wield it in your hand'.

The purpose here is not to examine the political, social and religious
situation that led to the creation of the *Khalsa*, but rather the consequences that this group had, and continues to have, on the Sikh
identity.

The *Khalsa* established Sikhism as a distinct religious movement,
and established a unique and separate Sikh identity (McLeod 1997,
pp. 47–61) defined by *amrit* (baptism), and the Five Ks (*panj
kakar*).

It is this order of 'soldier saints' as instituted by Guru Gobind
Singh that has become the model of a true Sikh: the devout Sikh. It
is this religious identity, which is promoted by the Shiromani Gurdwara Prabandhak Committee (SGPC), the organization responsible
for overseeing and managing the gurdwaras (Sikh places of worship). The religious identity will be considered in the next section,
with reference to definitions in the *Rehat Maryada* and Gurdwara
Acts.

Theological Identity

Regardless of a label, there are several practices that all Sikhs, whether
baptized or not, should follow since Sikhism is a religion based as
much on action as belief. The goal of all Sikhs is to break the endless
cycle of death and rebirth and to be reunited with God (Singh 1968,
p. 54). To achieve this one must follow the teachings of the Gurus,
control the five vices, eradicate ego and cease being a *manmukh*. Guru
Nanak, stressed that this was achieved by a Sikh who practised *nam
japna* (meditation on God's name), *kirat karna* (honest work) and
vand chakna (giving to those in need).

The most important of these practices is meditating on the name of
God (*nam simran*), which should be done 24 hours a day, if possible.

At a minimum, Sikhs are instructed to recite and meditate on *nam*. There are three specific prayers: a Sikh should wake before dawn and recite the *Japji*, in the evening recite the *Rahiras* and, finally, the *Sohilla* just before bedtime:

> One who calls himself a Sikh of the Guru, the True Guru, shall rise in the early morning hours and meditate on the Lord's name. (GGS, p. 305)

However, *nam simran* is much more than just reciting words; it is a transforming of personality through practice (Cole and Sambhi 1985, p. 94). By performing *nam simran* one evolves and becomes transformed through the eradication and control of all features associated with being a *manmukh*, such as *haumai* (ego) and the five vices.

A second key practice is that of charity. A Sikh is meant to give one-tenth (*daswandh*) of his or her income to the service of the *panth* (Cole and Sambhi 1990, p. 60). Alongside charity is the notion of honest living and serving others.

When an individual, through *nam simran* and *sewa*, has overcome ego and gone from being self-centred to God-centred, he or she is on the path to spiritual liberation and is called a *gurmukh*. The practices and actions that make someone a *gurmukh* were preached by all the Gurus and described in the Guru Granth Sahib. They can loosely be defined as an informal Code of Conduct for followers. As a result of the above practices and actions two types of Sikhs could be defined on the basis of spirituality:

- *Gurmukh* – an individual who is 'God Orientated' and spiritually awake, and
- *Manmukh* – a 'self-centred and materialistic individual', who follows his/her own mind and desires, without remembering God.

These principles of practice and action were advocated by Guru Gobind Singh, and he formalized them when he issued a formal *Rehat* (Code of Conduct) for Sikhs to follow (McLeod 1989b, pp. 23–42). The *Rehat* was linked to the *Khalsa*, and those not initiated by the Guru were deemed not to be Sikhs (Grewal 2008, p. 77).

After the death of Guru Gobind Singh a number of codes came into existence which claimed to portray the proper customs and codes of conduct for Sikhs, but not all of them were fully accepted by the majority of Sikhs due to apparent inconsistencies with Sikh teachings and principles as set out in the Guru Granth Sahib. However, in the early twentieth century, the Shiromani Gurdwara Prabandhak Committee (SGPC) drafted Sikh scholars and theologians to work on a standardized code of conduct based on previous codes, removing any inconsistencies with reference to Sikh teachings. This was finalized and approved in 1950 under the title of the Sikh *Rehat Maryada*, and has not been changed since. The 1950 *Rehat Maryada* defines a Sikh as any human being who faithfully believes in:

(i)   One immortal being
(ii) Ten Gurus, from Guru Nanak Sahib to Guru Gobind Singh Sahib
(iii) The Guru Granth Sahib
(iv) The utterances and teachings of the ten Gurus
(v)   The baptism bequeathed by the tenth Guru, and who does not owe allegiance to any other religion.

If we accept the above information as the definitive descriptor of Sikh identity, then we have arrived at an answer to the question 'who is a Sikh?' These principles of practice and action were inculcated into the *Khalsa*. They played an important role in the *Khalsa* identity, which Sikhs attained through *Amrit Sanskar* (baptism), a ceremony that initiates Sikhs into the *Khalsa*. Membership in this sacred order requires the adoption of the *panj kakar* (Five Ks). It was this identity that was promoted by the Singh Sabha movement[2] which sought to promote Sikhism in its 'pure' (*Khalsa*) form. They reinforced the doctrines of the Guru Granth Sahib and the *Khalsa* ideal with 'uncompromising zeal' (Grewal 2008, p. 144). The Singh Sabha Movement was succeeded by the Akali Movement, which was concerned with establishing Sikh control over Gurdwaras. It was because of the actions of this movement that ultimately resulted in the creation of the SGPC under the 1925 Sikh Gurdwara Act which reinforced the *Khalsa* identity as the norm. The Gurdwara Act of 1925 (Section 2(9)) defined a Sikh as follows:

A person who professes Sikh religion; if any question arises as to whether any person is or is not a Sikh, he shall be deemed respectively to be or not to be a Sikh according as he makes or refuses to make in such manner as the local government may prescribe the following declaration: I, solemnly affirm that I am

a Sikh; that I believe in the Guru Granth Sahib; that I believe in
the Ten Gurus and that I have no other religion.

This definition of a 'Sikh' was problematic because it meant in theory,
that no-one who lived before the tenth Guru could be a Sikh even
though he/she had full faith in the earlier nine Gurus. It was also
viewed to be problematic when determining whether a deceased person was a Sikh or not since they could not make the declaration. It
was also argued that someone who died prior to the Act could not
prove that they had professed the Sikh faith. The definition was therefore amended by the Sikh Gurdwaras (Amendment) Act, 1930 stating
that

> Sikh means a person who professes the Sikh religion or, in case
> of a deceased person, who professed the Sikh religion or was
> known to be a Sikh during his lifetime;

> If any question arises as to whether any living person is or is not
> a Sikh, he shall be deemed respectively to be or not to be a Sikh
> according as he makes or refuses to make in such manner as the
> State government may prescribe the following declaration:

> *I solemnly affirm that I am a Sikh, that I believe in the Guru
> Granth Sahib, that I believe in the Ten Gurus, and that I have no
> other religion.* (Takhar 2005, p. 24)

The declaration 'I have no other religion' is interesting, because on
the one hand it can act as an acknowledgement of the influences of
other faith traditions and customs on Sikhs. On the other hand, it
clearly implies that anyone who has faith in other religions or does
not believe that, after the Ten Gurus, the Guru Granth Sahib (and
not any living person) is the only Guru for Sikhs cannot be defined
Sikh. Under this definition, many denominations such as Namdharis,
Radhaswamis and Udasis did not qualify to be defined as Sikhs by
the Law Courts in India because they revered Human personalities
after the tenth Guru had bestowed the Guruship to the Guru Granth
Sahib in 1708.

What is clear, however, is that the definition of a Sikh within the
various Gurdwara Acts is a broad one, with no pronounced emphasis
on an outward form or initiation. The *Khalsa* observation therefore was not exactly enforced until 1950 with the *Rehat Maryada*

(Takhar 2005).[3] This *Rehat Maryada* is an amalgamation of new and old rules and regulations to direct the conduct and beliefs of a Sikh (Purewal 2000, Takhar 2005). Today, the *Rehat Maryada* is considered authoritative in defining who is a Sikh, with the *Khalsa* characterizations made known in the following statement:

> Any person who believes in God: in ten Gurus; in the Guru Granth Sahib and other writings of the Gurus, and their teaching; in the Khalsa initiation ceremony, and who does not believe in the doctrinal system of any other religion. (Cole and Sambhi 1990, p. 147)

The Delhi Gurdwara Act of 1971 reinforces this by stating that for the purpose of voting for the Delhi SGPC only those who have been initiated into the *Khalsa* can do so because they are deemed to be Sikh.

On the basis of the above, McLeod contends that a 'true Sikh will normally be a Sikh of the Khalsa' (1989b). This is an orthodox view, which echoes the views of the Panth's hierarchy: that the *Khalsa* identity is the 'Sikh ideal'. Many introductory textbooks of Sikhism seem to embrace this definition. It is at this point, however, that the overly simplistic definition has to be deconstructed, because the facts are far more complex. For example, McLeod (1989b) argues that there are implications for accepting the *Khalsa* model as the unequivocally definitive archetype of Sikh identity because it excludes Sikhs who 'claim to be Sikhs yet decline to observe the traditional code of the Khalsa' (p. 5).

Types of Sikhs

All religions experience a difference between what people *should do* and what people *actually do*, and this is true for Sikhs (Nesbit 2000). While *Khalsa* observance may provide immediate answers for identity, it is evident that today one archetypal Sikh identity does not exist, and cannot be argued for. Not all Sikhs are the same. Like many faiths there are several groups within the *Panth* (Sikh community), who are different due to their observance of the Five Ks.[4] Today, the level of observance has resulted in the creation of 'categories' of Sikhs; principally *Khalsa* or *amritdhari*, *keshdhari* (a new term) and *sehajdhari/mona* Sikhs (it is important to note that *mona* is also a recent term). These identities can be ranked according to observance (Nesbitt 2000):

- *Amritdhari – Khalsa* – initiated Sikhs or 'proper Sikhs'
- *Keshdhari* – those who keep the *kesh*, otherwise unshorn hair and are not initiated
- *Mona/Sehajdhari* – clean shaven Sikhs
- *Gora Sikhs* – Western converts[5]
- *Patit* – someone who may have taken *amrit* but has lapsed (Takhar 2005).

Amritdhari Sikhs

Amritdhari Sikhs are Sikhs who have been baptized into the Sikh faith and have joined the *Khalsa* brotherhood which was 'founded by Guru Gobind Singh in an impressive ceremony at Anandpur in 1699' (Cole and Sambhi 1990, p. 56), in which he defined the Sikh community in terms of a distinct Sikh identity, separate from Hinduism and Islam (Deol 2001). The *Khalsa* order is an acquired discipline through which Guru Gobind Singh established a military paradigm for Sikhs, but also provided a definition of an identity: a true Sikh is an *amritdhari* Sikh. To become an *amritdhari* Sikh one had to go through the initiation ceremony Guru Gobind Singh instituted, *Amrit Sanskar* (Rait 2005). Commentaries on the ceremony describe how the Guru chose five beloved ones (*Panj Pyare*) from a large gathering at Anandpur on *Baishaki*. Each belonged to a different caste, but through the ceremony merged together into the *Khalsa* brotherhood, and all were assigned a caste neutral surname, 'Singh' and 'Kaur'[6] and given the Five Ks. The Ks are five external symbols: *kesh* (unshorn hair),[7] *kangha* (a small wooden comb), *kara* (a simple steel bangle, which reminds a Sikh of his connection with God), *kachera* (cotton shorts/underwear, which reinforces moral values) and *kirpan* (a curved sword: *kirpa*-kindness and *an*-righteousness). These articles of faith mean that baptized Sikhs can be physically distinguished and identified as baptized Sikhs.[8] The four key prohibitions are

1. Abstain from cutting any hair.
2. Do not smoke or take any intoxicants.

3. Refrain from eating halal meat.
4. Never indulge in adultery. (Takhar 2005)

The creation of the *Khalsa* also added another dimension to Sikh identity: any Sikh who joined the *Khalsa* was to be regarded as a saint-soldier (*sant-siphai*).[9] The saintly character incorporates the traditional moral values of the religion and represents a peace-loving individual, while the soldier aspect demonstrates the resolve of Sikhs to uphold the social values of justice and freedom. Thus, in other words, the *amritdhari* Sikhs were the embodiment of the Sikh ideal, socially responsible and spiritually focused. As a consequence Sikh identity today is ostensibly modelled on the *Khalsa* (Kalsi 1992), which gives Sikhs a distinct and strong self-identity as members of the Sikh faith.

Keshdhari Sikhs

Keshdhari Sikhs until recently were the largest group within the three categories. *Keshdhari* Sikhs follow very similar practices to the *amritdhari* Sikhs; however, they do not adhere to 'orthodox' Sikh principles. The *keshdhari* Sikhs, while not being baptized, are committed to the Five Ks, especially unshorn hair, which somehow seems to imply that *keshdharis* observe *all* of the Five Ks (Tatla 2001). Tatla, however, reassesses this statement in Tatla and Singh (2006), changing the statement to 'most' of the Five Ks. A *Keshdhari* will uphold some of the Five Ks, but may still use his or her family/caste name. Alternatively they may go purely by the name of Singh/Kaur, but only uphold one or two of the Ks, mainly *kesh* and *kara*. The only unifying factor in '*keshdhari*' identity is that they all observe unshorn hair, hence the name '*keshdhari*' (Singh and Tatla 2006, p. 18). Some *keshdhari* Sikhs can also be referred to as *mona* Sikhs because there is an increasing trend to trim beards. This is particularly so among ramgarhia and jat caste Sikhs.

Mona/Sehajdhari Sikhs

Those who did not join the *Khalsa* in 1699 were seen as *sehajdhari* Sikhs – people who had not made the full commitment to the faith, but someday would, in other words, 'Sikhs in training' or 'slow adopters'. This view is still held by many Sikhs today. However, today *sehajdhari* is used interchangeably with the term *mona* Sikh, and both refer to Sikhs who cut their hair.

Mona or *sehajdhari* Sikhs in the past were numerically a small population within the Sikh community. However, today they are becoming numerically large. The name *mona* (shaven) indicates that they cut their hair and are easy in their attitudes to their faith, picking and choosing what practices they want to follow (Cole and Sambhi 1985, p. 126). They are considered to be within the Sikh community, but 'taking their time' in adopting the *Khalsa* identity.

Keshdharis and *mona* Sikhs wear the *kara,* which in a sense has become a cultural marker, identifying them as Sikh. *Mona* Sikhs, like *keshdhari* Sikhs, use the Kaur and Singh categories. For example, some use the *Khalsa* names of Singh and Kaur; others use only their family/caste names, while yet others use both, taking on the *Khalsa* name as a 'middle name'.

There is little acceptance, especially in the religious sphere, of *sehajdhari/mona* Sikhs by practising Sikhs (McLeod 1989b, Singh 2000, Tatla and Singh 2006). The element of practicality that surrounds Sikhism means that *sehajdhari* and *mona* Sikhs view themselves as Sikhs because they practice the religion according to the practical actions that the Gurus had introduced: *nam japna, kirat karna,* and *vand chakhna.* Those outside the community would probably recognize them as Sikhs on the grounds of ethnicity and actions, because, as in many Western traditions, one can have belief and faith without necessarily following all the practices as devoutly as one should.

Gora (White) Sikhs

The development of the Sikh Dharma of the Western Hemisphere or 'Happy, Healthy, Holy' (3HO)[10] movement in the United States, mainly located in New Mexico and Southern California, has also created an interest, and an anxiety around the question of Sikh identity.[11] The majority of *Gora* Sikhs are white, hence the name, who have converted voluntarily to Sikhism by taking *amrit*.[12] The *Gora* Sikhs place a strong emphasis on the *Khalsa* identity and the *Rehat Marayda*. Their identity, it is argued, is pure and true to Guru Gobind Singh's *Khalsa* identity and this raises problems for the Punjabi Sikhs because strict adherence and observance of the *Khalsa Rehat* poses a problem for Punjabi Sikhs. This is because Punjabi Sikhs, including those who have taken *amrit*, are inextricably linked to cultural practices, which the Gurus and the *Rehat Maryada* condemn; for example, caste affiliation. The *Gora* Sikhs observe the *Rehat* in its entirety and are not influenced by culture and religion. While some Punjabi Sikhs are known to admire the observance of the *Khalsa* discipline by the *Gora* Americans, most Punjabi Sikhs do not see them as 'real' Sikhs (Dusenberry 1988, Jakobsh 2008, Kalsi 1992) on the grounds of ethnicity – no Punjabi heritage because they have not been born into the Sikh faith. It is for this reason that many Punjabi Sikhs will not marry their children to a Sikh convert. Punjabi heritage is perceived to be a fundamental criterion of the Sikh identity by Sikhs (Jakobsh 2008, Takhar 2005, pp. 172–6).

Legal Identity

In the above sections we have discussed the theological definition, which is grounded in the teachings of the ten Gurus, of who a Sikh is, and how there is diversity within the community. In the following section we will look at recent legal definitions which have arisen due to court cases in the United Kingdom and Punjab, India: *Gurleen Kaur vs the State of Punjab, Mandla vs Dowell Lee* and *Sarika Watkins-Singh vs Aberdare Girls' School*. As we discuss the cases we will see how the definitions differ.

Gurleen Kaur vs the State of Punjab

The most important and current court case that provides a legal definition, which supports the theological definition provided by the *Rehat Maryada* and the various Gurdwara Acts is *Gurleen Kaur vs the State of Punjab*.

Gurleen Kaur was a *keshdhari* Sikh who had planned to attend the Sri Guru Ram Das Institute of Medical Sciences and Research in Amritsar. Gurleen was denied entrance into the college on the grounds that she plucked her eyebrows and was, as the college claimed, no longer a Sikh. The attorney for the college drew on the Sikh Gurdwara Act of 1925 and the Sikh *Rehat Maryada*, and argued that she had lapsed and become a *patit*. Who is a *patit*? *Patit* translates roughly as apostate and is the term given to individuals who were Sikhs but are now considered non-Sikh because they have gone against the Sikh teachings. The Gurdwara Act defines a *patit* as

> . . . a person who being a keshdhari Sikh trims or shaves his beard or keshas or who after taking amrit commits any one or more of the kurahits including disrespect to the hair. [Gurdwara Act of 1925, section 2(11)]

This has major implications for all Sikhs. By stating that a *patit* is a 'lapsed' *keshdhari/amritdhari*, it is implying something very clear: that a *keshdhari* Sikh must not cut his or her hair or (in the case of men) beards. The Gurdwara Act does not explicitly say that *sehajdhari* Sikhs must have unshorn hair, but the definition of a *patit* implies this: if *sehajdhari* Sikhs cut their hair they will be labelled a *patit*, a non-Sikh. In court, a Sikh cleric, Giani Harinder Pal Singh, claimed:

> Those who don't want to stay with Sikhism are free to leave, but once they leave, they shouldn't claim to be a Sikh and crave for a place in the religion. (*Times of India*, Vishal Sharma, 21 March 2009)

The court was trying to reconcile the distinct positions of Sikh identity with *kesh* (hair) as the religion's most recognized symbol and liberal interpretation of the religion's tenets. The decision of the court was to uphold the college's reasons for denying entrance; essentially agreeing that in order to be a Sikh, one must observe, at a minimum, *kesh* in its strictest interpretation. However, this definition inherits the limitations and problems that are associated with the *Khalsa* model, primarily its lack of recognition of the growing *mona* Sikh population. What is interesting is that this legal definition of a Sikh is primarily based on theology, something which the legal definitions in the United Kingdom are not.

Religious, Ethnic or Racial Identity?

While the Gurleen Kaur case in India was grounded in an identity based on religious beliefs and observed practices, as accorded by Guru Gobind Singh, there have been two important cases in the United Kingdom where the definition[13] of a Sikh is more than just a religious definition. There is an interesting parallel here with the question of

Jewish identity. Just as with Judaism and other religions there are religious and cultural components to Sikh identity. However, unlike other religions but similar to Judaism there appears to be a strong ethnic component attached to Sikh identity, and this has been emphasized by cases such as *Mandla vs Dowell Lee* and *Sarika Watkins-Singh vs Aberdare Girls' School*.

Mandla vs Dowell Lee

The case of *Mandla vs Dowell Lee* is often cited in discussions about the definition of Sikh identity. It set a precedent for the recognition of Sikhs in a legal setting in the diaspora of the United Kingdom. Singh and Tatla (2006) feel that it 'marked a major landmark in the development of the community and anti-discrimination legislation in Britain' (p. 130).[14]

The case centred on a Sikh student, who in 1978 sought admission to Park Grove School in Edgbaston, Birmingham. A. G. Dowell Lee, the school's headmaster, denied the student admission because he felt the turban was in violation of the institution's uniform policy. His father lodged a complaint with the Commission for Racial Equality, claiming that his son had been racially discriminated against.

The case went to the County Court[15] (*Mandla vs Dowell Lee* [1982] UKHL 7 (24 March 1982); [1983] 2 AC 548) where the central issue was whether Sikhs were a racial group within the meaning of the Race Relations Act 1976. The argument of race failed because, in the words of Lord Templeman (at p. 569),

> They are more than a religious sect; they are almost a race and almost a nation. As a race, Sikhs share a common colour, and a common physique based on common ancestors from that part of the Punjab which is centred on Amristar. They fail to qualify as a separate race because in racial origin prior to the inception of Sikhism they cannot be distinguished from other inhabitants of the Punjab.

Through the process of interpreting the legislative provisions in the Race Relations Act 1976, the court failed to recognize Sikhs as a 'racial group' because they were indistinguishable from other, non-Sikh, Punjabis, and decided that the turban was a religious symbol, rather than an ethnic symbol, and therefore Sikhs could not claim the right and protection to wear the turban under the Race Relations Act.

The CRE then took the case to the Court of Appeal, where Lord Denning upheld the original ruling, stating that:

> The statute in section 3(1) contains a definition of a 'racial group'. It means a 'group of persons defined by reference to colour, race, nationality or ethnic or national origins'. That definition is very carefully framed. Most interesting is that it does not include religion or politics or culture. You can discriminate for or against Roman Catholics . . . communists . . . the 'hippies' as much as you like, without being in breach of the law. But you must not discriminate against a man because of his colour or of his race or of his nationality, or of 'his ethnic or national origins'. You must remember that it is perfectly lawful to discriminate against groups of people to whom you object – so long as they are not a racial group. . . . No matter whether your objection to them is reasonable or unreasonable . . .

The CRE appealed to the House of Lords. In a speech with which Lord Edmund-Davies, Lord Roskill and Lord Brandon agreed (as they did with Lord Templeman), Lord Fraser of Tullybelton set out the factors to be considered in assessing whether a protected 'ethnic group' exists:

> For a group to constitute an ethnic group in the sense of the Act of 1976, it must, in my opinion, regard itself, and be regarded by others, as a distinct community by virtue of certain characteristics. Some of these characteristics are essential; others are not essential but one or more of them will commonly be found and will help to distinguish the group from the surrounding community. The conditions which appear to me to be essential are these, (1) a long shared history, of which the group is conscious as distinguishing it from other groups, and the memory of which it keeps alive; (2) a cultural tradition of its own, including family- and social customs and manners, often but not necessarily associated with religious observance. In addition to these two essential characteristics the following characteristics are, in my opinion, relevant, (3) either a common geographical origin, or descent from a number of common ancestors; (4) a common language,

not necessarily peculiar to the group; (5) a common literature peculiar to the group; (6) a common religion different from that of neighbouring groups or from the general community surrounding it; (7) being a minority or being an oppressed or dominant group within a larger community, for example (say, the inhabitants of England shortly after the Norman conquest and their conquerors might both be ethnic groups). A group defined by reference to enough of these characteristics would be capable of including converts, for example, persons who marry into the group, and of excluding apostates. Provided a person who joins the group feels himself or herself to be a member of it, and is accepted by other members, then he is, for the purposes of the Act, a member. . . . In my opinion, it is possible for a person to fall into a particular racial group either by birth or adherence, and it makes no difference, so far as the Act of 1976 is concerned, by which route he finds his way into the group. (*Mandla vs Dowell Lee* [1983] 2 AC at 562E)

In the course of his reasoning, Lord Fraser stated at p. 561D:

I recognize that 'ethnic' conveys a flavour of race but it cannot, in my opinion, have been used in the Act of 1976 in a strictly racial or biological sense.

Lord Fraser also stated that in seeking for the true meaning of 'ethnic' in the statute, the courts are not tied to the precise definition in any dictionary. He referred to the definition in the 1972 supplement to the *Oxford English Dictionary*: 'pertaining to or having common racial, cultural, religious or linguistic characteristics, esp. designation a racial or other group within a larger system . . . ' (Lord Fraser p. 562C).

The value of the 1972 definition is that it highlights how 'ethnic' has come to be commonly used in a sense appreciably wider than the strictly racial or biological definition. The word 'ethnic' still retains a racial flavour but it is used nowadays in an extended sense to include other characteristics which may be commonly thought of as being associated with common racial origin.

Thus, the definition of an 'ethnic group' was widened into a sociological definition (as well as a racial and biological one). Applying the above criteria, to the Mandla case meant that Sikhs constituted an 'ethnic group', and on 23 March 1983, the Law Lords overturned the decision and upheld the appeal. The Law Lords recognized the Sikh community as a separate race and ethnicity, rather than just a religious community, and therefore their right to be protected under the 1976 Act (Singh and Tatla 2006, p. 133).[16] Clearly this case was important for many Sikhs because being a Sikh becomes more than just a religious affiliation. If the *Mandla v Dowell Lee* judgement is used to define Sikh identity, then it can be argued that a Sikh is someone who belongs to a racial group and who is accepted by the UK government as a member of a distinct ethnic group. Therefore, from a social, rather than a religious, point of view a Sikh is anyone who is born into a Sikh family regardless of the religious beliefs and practices they follow. This legal 'label', however, is open to serious questions; questions which also apply to *Sarika Watkins-Singh vs Aberdare Girls' School.*

Sarika Watkins-Singh vs Aberdare Girls' School

The most recent legal case[17] involving the Sikh faith and identity was *Sarika Watkins-Singh vs Aberdare Girls' School.* The *Sarika/Kara* case raises some difficult questions when it is put in context with the *Gurleen Kaur vs the State of Punjab* case in India.

Sarika was a young British Hindu Punjabi girl by birth who had accepted her stepfather's Sikh identity. She was not a Sikh by birth, nor was she baptized Sikh, yet she had to defend her 'Sikh identity'.

School uniform policies of the Aberdare Girls' School bans any jewellery aside from wristwatches and plain ear studs. Under this policy Sarika was asked to remove her *kara* (steel bangle). Sarika refused and was excluded from school. Sarika brought a legal challenge against her school. The court ruled that the school was guilty of 'indirect discrimination under race relations' and equality laws.[18]

Justice Silber in his judgement said that the school had indirectly discriminated racially against her under the Race Relations Act and religiously under the Equality Act. Justice Silber accepted that for Sarika the *kara* was essential to her religious identity, and that she had been disadvantaged in not being allowed to wear it. He acknowledged that she had not been 'rebellious' in wanting to wear it, nor could wearing it be compared to wearing a flag, because that had no religious significance. The judge said that according to the evidence that had been given the *kara* was a sign that a Sikh was 'handcuffed by it to God'. It was not to be regarded as a piece of jewellery, but was something to which she attached 'exceptional importance'. 'It is in her mind one of the defining physical things of being a Sikh' as 'it signifies the eternity of life and the bond between a Sikh and his or her Guru'. She wore it on the wrist 'as a constant reminder to do good with the hands'. It was a religious symbol which both demonstrated and reminded Sikhs of their faith. While some news articles made reference to the *kara* as a religious symbol, the vast majority focused on Sarika Watkins-Singh's ethnicity (*The Times*, Frances Gibb, 30 July 2008, 'Sikh teenager Sarika Watkins-Singh wins right to wear bangle,' http://www.buisness.timeonline.co.uk/tol/business/law/article4425925.ece). Articles featured words such as 'Punjabi' and 'race', despite this being a case surrounding religious discrimination and a religious article of faith. What this demonstrated was that the terms 'Punjabi' and 'Sikh' have become interchangeable.

One of the newspapers reported that Sarika was an 'observant' Sikh, but did not define what this meant; for example, whether she was baptized or not. Sarika is not a baptized Sikh, and, although the *kara* is compulsory for a baptized Sikh, it is not for a non-baptized Sikh. Sarika Singh won her case because it was argued on the grounds of Religious and Racial Discrimination and not on the grounds of Freedom of Religion as debated in Article 9 of the European Convention on Human Rights: Freedom of Thought, Conscience and Religion.[19]

What the Sarika Watkins-Singh and Mandla cases demonstrate is that British law has taken a very different route than Indian law in choosing to classify Sikhs as an 'ethnic' rather than religious group. However, is this the right way to define a Sikh in the Diaspora? By classifying 'Sikh' as an ethnicity unintentionally the religious and spiritual symbolism of these articles of faith[20] appear to be 'denigrated' to cultural symbols/items. The concern with the Sarika Watkins-Singh case is also that the Five Ks may merely become an expression of cultural identity and become open to 'cultural misappropriation' by 'outsiders' who will adopt elements from the Sikh religious culture because they are 'cool', like a young non-Sikh Westerner carrying a *kirpan*, or a non-Sikh Westerner wearing the *kara*. If such misappropriation of Sikh articles of faith did occur, Sikhs would find this highly offensive. Importantly, with such rulings where do the *Gora* Sikhs belong? Are they entitled to the same treatment under the law?

Overall, what is clear from these cases is that while a theologically based definition of Sikhs as used by the State of Punjab is limiting and ignores the great diversity of observance within the Sikh community, the approach taken by the British courts is reductionist. The theological definition restricts the name 'Sikh' to those who strictly uphold the religious tenets, 'and alienates all other Sikhs who are not baptized', while the ethnicity definition reduces an entire religious movement to cultural practices. It is important to note that culture does play an important role in Sikh religious identity, and as a result the phenomenon of religion is central to the study of – culture – and vice versa and cannot be avoided responsibly (McLeod 1999).

Sikh Identity in the Diaspora

Sikhs are dispersed all over the world; destinations have largely been former British colonies (Dusenberry 1997). Approximately 5 per cent of Sikhs (between 1 and 1.25 million Sikhs) live overseas (Tatla 2005). As a result of this migration, Sikhism in the diaspora has become a composite religious experience; where Sikhs are negotiating multiple ways of being Sikh (Maira 1999, Nesbitt 2000). For the most part diaspora Sikhs are not *Khalsa* orientated (Nesbitt 2000). They affirm broader identities which have more to do with culture than religion.

In Sikh scholarship there has been considerable discussion about the conflict that arises through interaction between Sikh and non-Sikhs. Until recently, it had been argued that those in the diaspora are caught between two cultures, and that they were undergoing identity transformations (Takhar 2005). For many there was a potential 'identity crisis' and 'conflict' (Madan 1998), arising from the impact of Western traditions on traditional[21] religious and cultural identities (McLeod 1989a). Within the field of religious identity it is clear that in the 1960s and 1970s Sikh men on arrival into the United Kingdom cut their hair in the belief that this would make them more employable. Although this belief,which arises out of the fear of discrimination, does not exist today it is clear that the impact of Western traditions has been approached in different ways by young Sikhs, and this approach varies along the lines of baptized and non-baptized identity. While migration has not resulted in an erosion of Sikh religious values and teachings, certain external markers have been altered to meet the needs of the new environment in the last twenty years. For example, the external symbol of the turban covering the hair has been replaced by a baseball cap, or *keshdhari* men wearing their hair in ponytails. This could have something to do with discrimination and racism and wanting to minimize visibility (Nesbitt 2000), or it may just be that some Sikhs are rebelling or acting disaccorded and whimsical (Bradby 2007, Oberoi 1992). The *kara* is the only visible 'K' (Nesbitt 2000) all Sikhs wear and can be viewed as a cultural symbol rather than a religious symbol.

Young baptized Sikhs are not stuck between two cultures. Instead, they are strict observers of their religious tradition and they are often the ones who highlight discrepancies between teaching and practice. For example, they highlight how the teachings contained in the *Rehat Maryada* have become dominated or adapted by cultural practices and traditions, such as caste-based gurdwaras,[22] interfaith marriages, dowry giving (see Chapter 3) and caste endogamous marriages. These are practises which they see as going against Sikh teachings.[23] This was demonstrated in 2007 when young baptized Sikhs in Birmingham raised the issue of interfaith marriages taking place in gurdwaras. They argued that this should not happen (see Chapter 4, 'Ethics').

Many young baptized Sikhs also feel alienated and powerless in their religious community, and as a result forge a separate Sikh identity for themselves on the basis of observance. For example, many young baptized Sikhs (also non-baptized Sikhs) feel alienated from their gurdwaras because they have the perception that most gurdwara committees are made up of Sikh elders, mainly men, who are involved in political infighting,[24] and who do not wish to relinquish their control of gurdwaras in favour of either younger members or women.

Many Sikhs born in the diaspora are not baptized Sikhs, but they still define themselves as Sikh and have a certain amount of knowledge and understanding of their faith (Takhar 2005). These Sikhs believe that adhering to symbols does not make a good Sikh (Sidhu 1993). Instead, they argue that *practice* is what one should be concerned with. However, while this may be true, non-baptized Sikhs realize that they are not fully accepted by the baptized Sikh community. This has resulted in discrimination between the different types of Sikhs mentioned in this chapter, due to the hierarchy that has been created between baptized and non-baptized Sikhs. In many gurdwaras there is a strong emphasis on maintaining the *Khalsa* identity, that is, to take *amrit* and become baptized. Non-baptized Sikhs, particularly *mona* Sikhs are generally not looked on favourably. As a result some gurdwaras will not allow them to perform kirtan and some gurdwaras reserve committee roles and certain gurdwara duties only for baptized Sikhs. This has led to a certain alienation and disenchantment within the community, especially among *mona* Sikhs, which may explain the increasing popularity of non-orthodox 'pseudo-Sikh' religious sects and movements in India and abroad among this group.

Conclusion

This chapter highlights that the creation of the *Khalsa* has fashioned a consciousness of Sikh identity (McLeod 1989b). A 'Sikh image' was made and given meaning through the *Khalsa* (Bradby 2007). In marking boundaries, the *Khalsa* introduced ideas of a common ancestry, codified norms of obedience and ritualized the Sikh way of worship (Kaur 2001, Madan 1998, McLeod 1989a and b), and a practice developed whereby persons were categorized by their conformity to characteristics of 'Sikhness'.

The Sikh *Rehat Maryada* defines what it means to be a Sikh in the strict theological sense: one who upholds the *Khalsa* identity as laid down by Guru Gobind Singh. As a result, there is a tendency for members of the religious community, and even outsiders, to overemphasize the *Khalsa* identity. For example, many Sikh people in positions of religious authority will most likely be baptized Sikhs, and they will most likely dismiss the statement that anyone born to a Sikh couple is automatically a Sikh, because for religious Sikhs 'it is not birth which makes one a Sikh but illumination' (Cole and Sambhi 1985, p. 122), and illumination comes in the form of *amrit*. As a result, they view *Khalsa* Sikhs to be true Sikhs, willing to make any sacrifice for their faith, unlike 'other' (non-baptized) Sikhs, who are considered to be 'learners' or 'slow adopters', who hopefully will become 'true Sikhs'.

Through an analysis of Sikh practice, the Gurdwara Acts, *Rehat Maryada* and law cases, this chapter highlights how a definition of a Sikh grounded in baptism is too narrow. There is diversity within the *Panth*, in which there are several stages that define a person's religiosity, and which in turn affects his or her identity. These stages demonstrate diversity in observance, behaviour and actions, and hence there be an acknowledgement and acceptance of the existence of different types of Sikhs (Takhar 2005). Cole and Sambhi provide two definitions for who is a Sikh. The first is a person who holds certain beliefs, lives according to these and takes part in certain rites associated with them.

And the second is

someone who comes from a Sikh family, perhaps wears a turban, speaks Punjabi and is in a cultural sense a Sikh but has ceased to practice the religion. (Cole and Sambhi 1985, p. 106)

These simple statements clearly recognize the existence and difference between the religious Sikh and the cultural Sikh. McLeod also acknowledges this less religious Sikh; he identifies that it would be naïve to assume that all those who regard themselves as Sikhs would have a clear understanding of the religious doctrines or regularly follow religious practices, such as *nam simran*, in the same way that the vast majority of Christians have a limited knowledge and understanding of the Bible. By not making the theological *Khalsa* identity as given by Guru Gobind Singh a prerequisite to being defined a Sikh, there is an acknowledgement that there are Sikhs who do not conform to the *Khalsa* ideal, but who are Sikh through birth.[25] For example, according to McLeod, in times of peace and stability external demonstrations of faith are crucial, if one keeps one's hair uncut, refrains from smoking and identifies oneself as a Sikh for all 'practical purpose they will be regarded as Sikhs of the *Khalsa*' (McLeod 1989, p. 110). This implies that it is not necessarily the actual baptism ceremony that defines Sikhs as religious Sikhs, but the practices they uphold in their daily life. In certain circumstances religious Sikhs accept Sikhs who are not practising and encourage them to support their cause – for example, the calls for all Sikhs to demonstrate the 1984 Golden Temple Attack and the 2004 *Behzti* Affair in Birmingham, United Kingdom.

Hence, the term 'Sikh' should acknowledge that there are 'strict' and 'observant' Sikhs, as well as 'nominal Sikhs' and a plethora of individuals who exist somewhere between these two extremes. It also needs to be recognized that no one type of Sikh can claim a monopoly on Sikh identity; every Sikh can express very different possibilities for Sikhism and Sikh identity, and this can be informed by multiple factors. It is also clear that distinctions on the basis of religious observance – *amritdhari*, *keshdhari* and *sehajdharis* – have a damaging affect on Sikh identity because a hierarchy is established, and the original intent of the Gurus to create a unified Sikh identity appears to have become nullified. Acceptance of diversity would not be detrimental to the concept of 'Sikh identity'. Instead, it supports the strict theological definition of who is a Sikh by stressing that a Sikh is someone who is expected to treat all people equally, irrespective of caste, gender or creed, and that a Sikh is expected to adopt the Five Ks and join the *Khalsa* at some point in his or her life. By using the term 'expected' the 'preferred' model is identified, in essence, the '*Khalsa* Sikh'.

Chapter 6

Conclusion

To sum up, the main aim of this book was not to advance theory, but rather to describe and discuss in detail, on the basis of scriptural analysis, why and how a religious community behaves in an ever-changing world. Through the analysis of contemporary issues it is clear that Sikhs, who themselves had feared that living in the Diaspora and Modern World would eventually result in the loss of their religious teachings and cultural traditions, have not lost their religious identity or traditions. Sikhs have not chosen to 'do as the Romans do', such as assimilate and conform to the values of the 'host community'. Instead, they appear to have maintained a hold on to their religious teachings through a process of reinterpretation.

In this book I have outlined and explained the core religious beliefs, by exploring the writings and teachings of the ten Sikh Gurus in Sikhism's Holy Scripture, the Guru Granth Sahib. Although it was written between the fifteenth and seventeenth centuries ce, and hence within the context of this period, for Sikhs its teachings are seen as relevant today as they were back then. It is clear that the Guru Granth Sahib provides a methodology for achieving liberation/salvation and in doing so attempts to describe the nature of reality and God. At the same time, the Guru Granth Sahib provides some guidance about how one should live. The Guru Granth Sahib contains a number of verses stressing the importance of living a moral life whilst living the life of a 'householder'. The significance of these verses is that they were written against a backdrop of belief that asceticism was necessary to connect with God and that liberation was open to men only. It could also be argued that in stressing the importance of family, the Gurus also attempted to raise the position of women in society. In any case, it is clear from the Guru Granth Sahib that spiritual liberation is open to men and women equally.

While the Sikh community's traditional and cultural practices have always been varied and hybrid (Ballard 1994; Singh and Tatla 2006), the basic principles of the religion have been maintained. This does not mean that teachings, traditions and practices are followed to the letter or through 'blind faith'. Whilst there is a blind acceptance of the Guru Granth Sahib, the interpretation of teachings have not remained fixed. Instead, it is evident that the Sikh community in India, as well as in other transnational areas of Sikh settlement, are having to accommodate advances in a dynamic and ever-changing world, and as a result is having its religious beliefs questioned critically in a modern context.

This book has attempted to outline major modern issues that are confronting the Sikhs, and how the Guru Granth Sahib in its role as the 'Eternal Guru' and perpetual guide for all Sikhs addresses modern issues such as gender inequality, advances in science and technology, family life and homosexuality. It is clear that the Sikh community is employing an ongoing strategy of interpretation and reinterpretation of the teachings from the Guru Granth Sahib to accommodate the changes that are occurring in society, but this will not lead to an abandonment, changing or impoverishment of the religious teachings. The religious teachings have been, and will continue to be, successfully maintained in their original form. Instead, we are seeing a challenge and readdressing of modern issues through a critical engagement with the religious texts. Teachings have been analysed and reinterpreted from various perspectives, such as Western feminism and scientific perspectives. While some reinterpretations may seem deceptively radical, a closer examination reveals an essential continuity in religious beliefs.

It will only be through this process that the religion will be able to manage and tackle modern-day issues, and this will not lead to a new way of being Sikh, but will lead to someone being a Sikh who is equipped to deal with modern issues according to the Guru Granth Sahib.

No reinterpretation of the Guru Granth Sahib is precisely the same, and there is no single definitive interpretation. Every reading and interpretation can be viewed as a new creative act unique to the individual. This is evident when Sikhs are making decisions at a personal level and are using the Guru Granth Sahib to make ethical decisions for themselves through a personal understanding. Interpretations are always different, and this difference is dependent on a number of issues, such as gender, age, whether the individual is baptized or not, level of education or even where one lives. For example, Sikhs in India and in the diaspora, whether in Britain, America or Canada, will have different interpretations of the core religious text when answering questions about modern issues, such as genetic engineering, IVF, homosexuality, marriage and 'Who is a Sikh?'

While it is clear from Chapters 2, 3 and 4 that religion guides behaviour, it is also clear from them that behaviour is governed by culture, especially notions of *izzat* (honour). While religious teachings may be reinterpreted, cultural values cannot and for this reason are prescriptive, and do prevent, change. For example, when Sikhs hear the term 'homosexuality' or 'genetic engineering' many automatically associate them with something negative, but today the influence of Western culture and education has encouraged some Sikhs to become more 'liberal' in their thinking. Like other religious traditions there are two schools of thought – Conservative and Liberal – which are influenced by religion and culture. For example Conservative Sikhs argue that because the Guru Granth Sahib only describes a monogamous relationship between a man and woman then homosexuality is forbidden by God. Liberal Sikhs argue that since the Guru Granth Sahib stresses the importance of respect and equality, this should be accorded to homosexuals. However, culturally, notions of *izzat* (honour) and shame will be invoked to prevent any deviation from the norm – marriage – and a radical reinterpretation of the text will be viewed as a misinterpretation.

Chapter 2 focuses on science – advances that have been made and the implications these have had for Sikh ethics. In the chapter, it becomes clear that there are a variety of interpretations of religious teachings to accommodate changes in the practices surrounding conception and childbirth. The maintenance of Sikh religious values and traditions relating to marriage, sex, conception and childbirth, for example, certain scientific advances and Western practices and values relating to sex and childbirth, have been legitimatized through a reinterpretation of religious teachings which, however, have remained the same. The most prominent example is childbirth and IVF. In the past it would have been argued that it was one's *karma* that one could not have children and that one should accept God's *hukam* (will). However, today many Sikhs will argue that God has provided humankind with the capacity to think and reason and that it is indeed God's *hukam* for humans to use our God-given brains to develop technology so that it may ease suffering and pain which many childless couples experience. It is clear from the example of IVF that, contrary to the expectations of some, there are Sikhs who are prepared to reinterpret the teachings in the Guru Granth Sahib to suit their needs. In this situation this process of interpretation and reinterpretation has become necessary for some Sikhs so that they can fulfil not only the cultural, but also the religious requirement of marriage and having children. However, we need to note that there is an abuse of the practice, especially in the realm of pre-implantation genetic diagnosis.

For the religious community IVF has not been without consequences. It raises questions, similar to those raised by other religious communities: Would single women or gay couples use the technology? Would it be okay for a couple to create and save excess embryos to be used in later attempts if the first try failed? IVF has also opened the door to new controversial concepts: 'saviour babies', born to save a sibling; 'designer babies', carrying certain selected genes; pre-implanatation genetic diagnosis, which allows the possibility of choosing the baby's sex; and human cloning.

Although there has not been an open discussion it is clear that Sikhs in private can debate the usefulness of new medical technology, embrace its benefits, but also abuse those benefits to meet cultural expectations.

It is also important to note (Chapter 2) how on the one hand, advances in the scientific arena and their acceptance are an interference in God's will, and on the other hand, that they are 'normal' and are all due to God's *hukam* (will). The aim of that chapter was to show the numerous ways of dealing with advances in science and society by Sikhs in the diaspora and India, and also to show how Sikh society functions, with reference to the Guru Granth Sahib that guides individuals and families to do the 'right thing'. There is unlikely to be one standard interpretation of the teachings since interpretations are determined by a variety of factors, such as age, gender, socioeconomic environment, but also personal circumstances, such as illness or poverty. The concept of individuality and personal decision making makes one question whether there is a need for a single interpretation, or whether a number of interpretations should be allowed. This is a question for the religious community to address.

Having discussed the changes that have occurred in the realm of science and society it became clear in the preceding chapters that the Sikh religion cannot be demarcated from culture. However, accommodating religious beliefs and practices with modern cultural practices and expectations will be difficult. The challenge today lies in reforming Sikh cultural values because they cross into religion. For example, gender inequality in the cultural arena crosses into the realm of religion, especially with reference to women's position in the gurdwara. How many Sikh women are the presidents of a gurdwara?

How many women do we see speaking about Sikhism on TV or radio? How many Sikh women have become gurdwara committee members, and if they have do they actually have a voice? When will we see women in the *panj pyare*? Or when will women be allowed to do *sewa* in the Harmandar Sahib complex? Long-established religious traditions may seem inappropriate and outdated today, and there can be an argument for change; however, it is clear that this is unlikely to happen any time soon due to male patriarchy and dominance.

If we take the example of gender inequality, it is clear that Sikhism does not just have a single view on women's role and position in the religious domain; rather, Sikhs interpret this issue in different ways depending on their circumstances. As a result, there are a variety of Sikh communities that have arisen due to their own interpretation of the Guru Granth Sahib with reference to gender. The Sikh Dharma of the Western Hemisphere (3HO) is one. It allows women to be part of the *panj pyare*, which promotes the equality that was preached by the Gurus.

Variation, though, is not always conducive and can lead to schisms, especially around issues such as homosexuality and gender inequality. For example, many Sikhs, born into the faith and ethnically Punjabi, including women, view the inclusion of women in the *panj pyare* by the 3HO organization to be wrong. Thus, does having lots of diverse groups strengthen Sikhism? Is a single interpretation, which seems true to the religious teachings necessarily a good thing? These are questions for future research.

In Chapter 4, issues surrounding ethics and morals are discussed. In that chapter, issues surrounding homosexuality and abortion highlight that while the written word within the Guru Granth Sahib cannot be altered in any way, this does not mean that it has not been manipulated through reinterpretation in certain instances to answer controversial modern-day issues, and in turn accommodate the new socio-environment the community is in. Homosexuality, same-sex marriages and adoption rights for gay couples will most certainly cause divisions within the community and are unlikely to get a clear consensus. This is clearly emphasized with reference to the incident in Canada in 2005 regarding the Gay Marriage Bill (see Chapter 4 for discussion). Sikhs who attempt to confront such problematic issues will not get far with reinterpreting core religious concepts to justify and support their position. For in this instance to reinterpret the eternal word of the Guru will be tantamount to changing the message of God.

While religion dictates what will happen with reference to such issues, so does culture. Sikhs are aware that by behaving in a 'modern' or 'progressive' way, such as adopting certain Western social and cultural conventions, they may be seen to be 'loose' and un-Sikh-like and this will bring dishonour to them. The concept of *izzat* ensures conformity. Inducing guilt is one way for parents to get what they want. For example, comments such as: 'You are a bad Sikh. Why are you doing this to me? Do you want to kill me?' can persuade children to return to the family fold, especially where homosexuality may be an issue. Thus, it is clear that while the immediate and extended family may be supportive, it can also be domineering and oppressive when it comes to protecting its honour (*izzat*). As a result, most Sikhs willingly retain their cultural and religious heritage.

Chapter 5 described different interpretations of 'Who Is a Sikh'. This was looked at from the religious perspective, such as practices, then the introduction of the *Khalsa* and finally a legal definition of 'Who is a Sikh'. While revealing the maintenance of Sikh religious values and traditions relating to the *Khalsa* identity, it showed how certain religious views/interpretations of identity have been manipulated to suit the needs of Sikhs in the diaspora.

Overall, for Sikhs it is important that they conform to the religion's teachings. Following religious 'tradition' increases and maintains one's identity and *izzat*. However, although most Sikhs feel they have to do what the religion has prescribed, some have manipulated and reinterpreted the teachings to suit their particular needs. For example, while the majority of second-, third- and fourth-generation Sikhs are adamant that they are not prepared to abandon their religious heritage, they have also made it that they are not prepared to have a religious heritage which is unwilling to accommodate their needs, many of which are new and an outcome of their dual socialization and modernity. It is this desire to maintain their religious traditions and simultaneously get what they want from this modern world that has to encourage Sikhs to work together to interpret religious teachings so that they accommodate the modern world.

All this demonstrates that the Guru Granth Sahib continues to underlie the entire Sikh social organization, and is the principal influencer when educating and determining an individual's basic roles and behaviour. New traditions and Western practices, but also scientific advances which may go against the teachings contained in the Guru Granth Sahib, such as contraception and genetic engineering, have not eroded or changed the core teachings: religious tenets and teachings have remained the same. Instead, the teachings have been interpreted in such a way to help answer modern-day concerns because Sikhs wish to retain their religious identity, and in turn their status within the community. Not many Sikhs will reinterpret the core concepts of the faith in ways that would seem to depart markedly from the teachings contained within the Guru Granth Sahib.

Thus, Sikhs are active producers and maintainers of their religion rather than passive products of it, and they have lived, and will continue to live the 'right' way by reinterpreting the Guru Granth Sahib without changing the core Sikh teachings. This will be an ongoing process for the Sikh community well into the twenty-first century.

Glossary

Akal purakh	God who is Beyond Time or is Timeless
akhand path	A continuous 48-hour reading of the Guru Granth Sahib (GGS) by the *granthi*
amrit	Holy water/nectar of immortality
ardas	The prayer that forms the culmination of any religious service
asa di var	Guru Nanak's morning prayer, consists of *Slokas* and 24 *Pauris*. It contains verses by Guru Nanak, Guru Angad, Guru Ram Das and Guru Arjan (GGS, pp. 462–75)
atma	Soul
Dasam Granth	A book containing the writings of Guru Gobind Singh
daswandh	Giving one-tenth of one's income to the service of the community
Gora Sikh	A Western convert to Sikhism
granthi/giani	A Sikh priest
gurdwara	A Sikh temple
gurmukh	Someone who has realized God and has overcome his/her ego
Guru Granth Sahib (GGS)	The Eternal Guru of the Sikhs. A sacred text that contains the compositions of the Sikh Gurus, as well as those of Hindu saints. It is at the centre of all Sikh worship
Haumai	Ego – I-I. Self-centredness, which prevents an individual from becoming a *gurmukh*

hukam	The will of God
Hukamnama	The culmination of the wedding ceremony with the reading of a verse from the Guru Granth Sahib chosen at random
kachera	A pair of cotton shorts, worn as one of the Five Ks
kangha	A small wooden comb, worn as one of the Five Ks
kara	A steel bangle, worn as one of the Five Ks
karah prasad	A sacrament. A sweet mixture which is made of equal amounts of flour, sugar, water and butter. It is placed in the cupped palms of the members of the congregation at the end of any religious service
Kaur	Literally, 'princess'. The surname given to all Sikh women of the *Khalsa*. It was introduced by Guru Gobind Singh to eliminate caste distinctions
kesh	Uncut hair, worn as one of the Five Ks
Khalsa	Literally, 'pure ones', the fellowship of Sikhs founded by Gobind Singh, the tenth Guru, in 1699
kirat karna	Honest work
kirpan	Sword, worn as one of the Five Ks
kirtan	Religious singing
langar	The community kitchen in the gurdwara. The meals in the gurdwara are cooked by women and served by men. Men and women eat separately. The men sit on one side of the room, while the women sit on the other side
lavan/lam	The four verses read at a wedding as the couple circumambulate the Guru Granth Sahib
manmukh	An individual who is ego orientated
maya	Greed or wealth
Nam simran/japna	Meditation on God's name
Nimrata	Humility
pahul	Initiation ceremony (baptism)

panj kakar	The Five Ks: five items each beginning with 'K', which members of the *Khalsa* wear
panj pyare	Literally, the 'five beloved'. The name given to the five men who were prepared to give up their faith. They were the first five members of the *Khalsa*
Panth	Sikh brotherhood
Parmatma	God
patit	A baptized Sikh who has lapsed in his/her observations. Today this term is also used to refer to Sikhs who are not baptized and do not live according to the *Rehat Maryada*
Rehat Maryada	Code of Conduct
sangat	Congregation
sanyog	Destiny
Satguru	God
sewa	Service
Shiromani Gurdwara Prabandhak Committee (SGPC)	Responsible for maintenance of the religion, but also the gurdwaras in Haryana and Punjab, India
sikhya	Moral teachings given by an elder
Singh	Literally, 'lion-hearted'. The surname given to all Sikh men of the *Khalsa*. It was introduced by Guru Gobind Singh to eliminate caste distinctions
vand chakna	Giving to those in need
Waheguru	Name by which Sikhs refer to God – Wonderful Lord

Appendix

Translation of the Marriage Hymns

Lavan – A Way of Living

The Guru Granth Sahib is a religious book containing the teachings of the Gurus on how one should live and behave on earth if union with God in the afterlife is to be achieved. The principal teachings of how one should behave on earth, and how union with God or one's spouse can be achieved, is explained in the four marriage hymns (Guru Granth Sahib, pp. 773–4). The circumambulation of the Guru Granth Sahib is a public demonstration of the couple's acceptance of the teachings of the Gurus.

This is the translation of the four wedding verses according to Wylam (n.d.).

The four verses represent the four stages of love: **first,** the preparation and justification for the state of marriage, which is encouraged and supported as the best state of life for a Sikh. It repudiates the idea that a religious person who dedicates his life to God should remain single. The **second** verse describes the first feeling of love when the bride has left her old life behind and begins the new life of partnership with her husband. The **third** verse describes the bride's (or the soul's) detachment from the world and outside influences, when she becomes more deeply devoted to her husband and wishes to live only for him. The **last** verse tells of the most perfect love and devotion when no feeling of separation is possible between the two. On the purely spiritual plane, it would be as if the soul has reached complete union with God and has found perfect joy in His love (Wylam n.d., p. 3).

Lavan – *The Marriage Hymn of Guru Ram Das*
(Arrangement by P. M. Wylam)

(1) In the first round,[1] the Lord ordains for you a secular life.
Accept the Guru's word as your scripture
And it will free you from sin.
Let your law of life be to meditate on the Name of God
Which is the theme of all scriptures.
Contemplate the true Guru, the perfect Guru
And all your sins shall depart.
Fortunate are those who hold God in their hearts;
They are ever serene and happy.
The slave Nanak declares that in the first round,
The marriage rite has begun.

(2) In the second round, the Lord has caused you to meet the true
Guru.
The fear in your hearts has departed
And the filth of egoism has been washed away.
Imbued with the fear of God and by singing His praises,
You behold His very presence.
The Lord God is the Soul of the Universe
And His presence pervades every place.
Within and without is the One God
And in the company of the saints the songs of joy are sung.
The slave Nanak proclaims that in the second round,
The divine strains of ecstasy are heard.

(3) In the third round, love for the Lord stirs in the heart
And the mind becomes detached from worldly things.
Through the company of the saints and by the great good
fortune,
I have met the Lord.
I have found the Immaculate Lord by singing His praises
And uttering His hymns.
Good fortune has brought me into the company of saints
Where tales of the Ineffable are told.
My heart is now absorbed in the Name of God
In accordance with the destiny written for me.
The slave Nanak declares that in the third round,
Divine love and detachment are born in the heart.

(4) In the fourth round, divine knowledge awakes in the mind
And union with God is complete.
Through the Guru's instruction the union is made easy.
And the sweetness of the Beloved pervades my body and soul.
Dear and pleasing is the Lord to me
And I remain ever absorbed in Him.
By singing the Lord's praises
I have attained my heart's desire.
God has completed this marriage
And the bride's heart rejoices in His Name,
The slave Nanak proclaims that in the fourth round,
You have obtained God as the Everlasting Bridegroom.
(Wylam n.d., pp. 5–6)

Altogether the verses inform the bride and groom of their duties to each other. The husband is to love and respect his wife, and recognize her individuality and equality as a human being and life partner. The wife achieves complete union through her love and respect for her husband, whether it be in affluence or adversity.

However, it is also clear that through the recital of the *lavan* the *Anand Karaj* (wedding ceremony) becomes an 'ideal spiritual marriage' (Narain Singh 1978). This is because the *lavan* suggests that the relationship formed through marriage is analogous to the relationship between God and the devotee.

Thus, marriage for the Sikhs is a 'union of the divine spark', rather than first a civil or social contract. The Spiritual Marriage, between the *atma* (soul, the bride) and the Supreme *Parmatma* (God, the spouse), is expressed figuratively as a union between the bride and bridegroom. This is because both unions have a common aim: while the soul needs to unite with God for fulfilment, the husband and wife need to pull together in mind, intellect, heart and spirit, to produce harmony and happiness during their life.

This is a very brief look at the implications and meanings of the hymns sung at the marriage ceremony.

Notes

Preface

1 Singh and Tatla (2006, p. 2) in their book *Sikhs in Britain* state that 336,000 Sikhs live in *Britain*.
2 Both the Guru Granth Sahib and the *Dasam Granth* are widely available and accessible through English translations. There are various English translations of the Guru Granth Sahib and *Dasam Granth* available on the internet, including www.sikhitothemax.com, www.sridasamgranth.com and www.search*Gurbani*.com. An English translation of the Guru Granth Sahib by Dr. Gopal Singh (1978) was used, and for the *Dasam Granth*: *Sri Dasam Granth Sahib. Text and Translation* (1999) by Dr. Jodh Singh and Dr. *Dharam* Singh was used.
3 The daughter of Guru Angad married the nephew of Guru Amar Das. There is no reference to the husband's name in the Sikh literary sources.

Chapter 1

1 Many Sikhs will wait to be baptized on *Baisakhi* day.
2 The word 'Gurdwara' can be broken down: *Gu*/darkness, *ru*/light and *Dwara'*/ abode or 'gateway' to the Guru. The Guru leads someone from spiritual ignorance into spiritual enlightenment (*ru*/light).

Chapter 2

1 www.sikhphilosophy.net/books-on-sikhism/23961-creation-universe-expounded-guru-nanaks-hymns.html, accessed 27 December 2010. www.sikhphilosophy.net/sikh-sikhi-sikhism/23702-origin-

life-evolution-according-science-gurbani.html, accessed 27 December 2010. www.esikhs.com/articles/Sikh_Religion.pdf, accessed 27 December 2010.

2 In Sikh scripture, the womb is often described as a dismal, frightening and hellish place.

3 Ten Indian months.

4 This scenario mirrors the case of Diane Blood, who sought permission from the courts to be inseminated with her dead husband's sperm. Her husband caught meningitis in February 1995 shortly after they had been trying to start a family. He lapsed into a coma and died before agreeing in writing for his sperm to be used (http://news.bbc.co.uk/onthisday/hi/dates/stories/february/6/newsid_2536000/2536119.stm, accessed on 8 June 2008). On 27 February 1997, the Human Fertilisation and Embryology Authority (HFEA) ruled Diane Blood should be allowed to export her dead husband's sperm as long as she attended a fertility clinic in Brussels. She claimed victory in her legal battle to have her late partner legally recognized as the father of her children in February 2003.

Chapter 3

1 Guru Nanak contradicts these teachings because according to the *Janam-sakhis* of the *Puratan* tradition he left his family for 30 years to travel in pursuit of the knowledge of God. As a result of this it is not clear when he realized the importance of family – was this before he left on his travels or after he had completed them?

2 There is a tendency to generalize Hindu textual views on women and other matters. Manu is sometimes seen as representative of the entire Hindu tradition. Certain practices such as *sati* did take place, but it was not prevalent in all parts of India, and therefore when we focus on the Gurus and their comments regarding the position of women, they have to be contextualized with reference to fifteenth-century Punjab. Just like in Sikhism, there is a diversity of textual views in Hinduism.

3 Pruthi and Sharma (1995, pp. 14–15) view this verse negatively. They feel that there is too much emphasis on the role of women as a mother and wife. They also ask why there is a focus on the fact that she will give birth to 'Kings'; then what about Queens. Doris Jakobsh also thinks that this *Shabad* portrays women as procreators who are valued if they produce Kings, and as a result this reinforces the

cultural preference for males. Jakobsh (2003) also argues that the Guru Granth Sahib's portrayal of the female is one sided and promotes subjugation to the male master hidden in the form of a male Guru. However, we have to keep in mind the historical context and time that the Guru Granth Sahib was written in. As a result of history, many practising Sikhs ignore the feminism of the Gurus' *bani* and how it does try to uplift women.

4 Guru Nanak Nishkam Sewak Jatha (GNNSJ) is a non-political, non-profit making, religious charitable organization committed to the selfless service of humanity. It has Gurdwaras in the United Kingdom (Birmingham, London and Leeds), Kericho, Kenya and India (Gurray and Anandpur in Punjab and Hazoor Sahib, Nanded). It has been led by three men: Sant Baba Puran Singh of Kericho (founder), Bhai Sahib Bhai Norang Singh and currently Bhai Sahib Mohinder Singh (Takhar 2005).

5 www.sikhsentinel.com/sikhsentinel0303/sikhwomen.htm, and http://fateh.sikhnet.com/s/sevaupdates.

6 Demands for dowry can go on for years. Religious ceremonies and the birth of children often become the occasions for further requests for money or goods.

7 Human Rights barrister, Usha Sood, represented a young Sikh woman, Dwinderjit Kaur, from Nottingham who after suffering dowry abuse under the guise of domestic violence sued her in-laws in 1997 and retrieved her dowry through the civil court.

8 The anti-dowry laws in India were enacted in 1961 but both parties to the dowry – the families of the husband and wife – are criminalized. The laws themselves have done nothing to halt dowry transactions and the violence that is often associated with them.

9 Sex selection and sex-selective abortion are not unique to Sikhs in Punjab and in the Diaspora. Amartya Sen (1992 and 2003) began writing about the issue of 'Missing Women' in the 1990s. This practice is prevalent among the Sikh, Hindu and Muslim communities in India and Pakistan, but also the Diaspora, but is also prevalent in countries like China (Sen 1992 and 2003). In his 1992 article he discusses the issue of female mortality through disadvantage etc., while in his 2003 article he discusses how while female mortality has been reduced substantially this has been counterbalanced by a new female mortality – that in natality – through sex specific abortions aimed against the female foetus.

10 India introduced the Pre-natal Diagnostic Techniques (Regulation and Prevention of Misuse) Act in 1994. It was supposed to regulate

the use of prenatal diagnostic techniques and prevent the misuse of such techniques for the purpose of prenatal sex determination:

> Sec. 6 of the 1994 Act, clearly states that the determination of sex is prohibited:
> 6. Determination of sex prohibited. On and from the commencement of this Act,

> (a) no Genetic Counselling Centre or Genetic Laboratory or Genetic Clinic shall conduct or cause to be conducted in its Centre, Laboratory or Clinic, prenatal diagnostic techniques including ultrasonography, for the purpose of determining the sex of a foetus;
> (b) no person shall conduct or cause to be conducted any prenatal diagnostic techniques including ultrasonography for the purpose of determining the sex of a foetus.

Further **Section 23.** *Offences and penalties* states: (1) Any medical geneticist, gynaecologist, registered medical practitioner or any person who owns a Genetic Counselling Centre, a Genetic Laboratory or a Genetic Clinic or is employed in such a Centre, Laboratory or Clinic and renders his professional or technical services to or at such a Centre, Laboratory or Clinic, whether on an honorary basis or otherwise, and who contravenes any of the provisions of this Act or rules made thereunder shall be punishable with imprisonment for a term which may extend to three years and with fine which may extend to ten thousand rupees and on any subsequent conviction, with imprisonment which may extend to five years and with fine which may extend to fifty thousand rupees. (THE PRE-NATAL DIAGNOSTIC TECHNIQUES (REGULATION AND PREVENTION OF MISUSE) ACT, 1994 ACT NO. 57 OF 1994 [20th September, 1994]: india.gov.in/allimpfrms/allacts/1623.pdf, accessed 26 April 2009).

11 CHAPTER X: Beliefs, Observances, Duties, Taboos and Ceremonies Article XVI Living in Consonance with Guru's Tenets: *The Sikh code of religious conduct*, published by Shiromani Gurdwara Prabandhak Committee (SGPC), 1950.

Chapter 4

1 Hell is not regarded as a physical place for Sikhs, but is a state of being trapped in the cycle of rebirth and death.
2 To describe detachment in the Guru Granth Sahib the Gurus used

the Indian imagery of the lotus flower.

> As the lotus lives detached in water, as the duck floats carefree on the stream, so one crosses the sea of material existence with the mind attuned to the Word. Live detached, shorn of hope, living in the midst of hope. (GGS, p. 938)

3 *Sangat* – religious congregation.
4 *Pangat* – people sitting together in rows to share a communal meal, i.e. *langar*.
5 *Sannyas* – renunciation, which was only open to men.
6 Having travelled far and wide to spread the message of *Nam*, Guru Nanak returned to his family and founded the city called Kartarpur (City of God), where he spent the last 18 years of his life during which he practiced *nam japna* in the context of his family. Guru Nanak put into practice his belief that one did not have to renounce family and worldly possessions to find God. He did this to restore the status of the family and to emphasize the importance of worshipping and performing *sewa* within the community. Guru Nanak through his teachings was able to stress that connecting with God depended more on one's morality and conduct in life (Jhutti-Johal 2007, p. 49).
7 The importance of monogamy in Sikhism may be questioned when we read that Guru Gobind Singh may have had between two and three wives: Mata Jito, Mata Sundri and Mata Sahib Kaur. However, much controversy exists around this assertion. Some Sikhs argue that he was actually only married to Mata Jito Ji, and that the other 2 women lived within his 'court' in his care. Others suggest that he was married to Mata Jito and Mata Sundri but not to Mata Sahib Kaur, who was known as the Mother of the *Khalsa* (Jakobsh 2003, pp. 38–9; Singh, Nikky 2005b, pp. 52–3). Sikhs would generally put this issue in to an historical context but today follow their 'Eternal Guru' the Guru Granth Sahib on the matter and not practice polygamy. Monogamy is the norm and encouraged
8 *Izzat* should be interpreted as honour of the family rather than just the honour of the individual.
9 *The Tribune*, Chandigarh, Wednesday, 16 May 2007, www.tribuneindia.com/2007/20070516/main6.htm (accessed 28 July 2009).

10 Forms of contraception: birth control implants, intra-uterine devices (coils), the morning after pill and the contraceptive pill.

11 Sikh mothers are told to mediate on God's name.

12 Sex selection and sex-selective abortion are not unique to Sikhs in Punjab and in the Diaspora. The latter practice is prevalent among the Hindu and Muslim communities in India and Pakistan, but also the Diaspora, and is also prevalent in countries like China (Sen 1992 and 2003).

13 While aborting a foetus with a disability goes against the religious teachings of *karam* and *hukam*, it also sends out a wrong message to the community, that is, that people with a disability are not equal or valued by society.

14 The *Akal Takht* (Seat of the Immortal One) was established by Guru Hargobind Singh (sixth Guru). Its role is to provide guidance to the Sikh community through '*hukamnamas*' (edicts).

15 'World Sikh group against gay marriage bill', CMC *News*, 29 March 2005, and Martin Regg Coh, '*Reject the gay bill, Sikh MPS told; Warning from top religious authority says marriage backers will be shunned*', Toronto *Star*, 28 March 2005.

16 Liberal views and discussions about homosexuality are prominent on the Internet (http://www.sarbat.net).

17 The four wedding verses composed by Guru Ram Das, the fourth Guru. They are read out once by the priest while the couple is seated and is then sung. When it is sung the couple walk around the Guru Granth Sahib. The *Lavan* came into force in 1909 when the Anand Marriage Act was introduced. Prior to that Sikhs married according to Hindu tradition – the circumambulation of the fire.

18 Marriages of convenience do happen, and this is clear from discussions boards such as Sarbat.Net Discussion Board – BRITISH GAY JATT SIKH GUY WANTED FOR MOC (http://sarbat.proboards.com/index.cgi?board=general&action=display&thread=187).

19 Sikhs rarely see portrayals of lesbian and gay Sikhs in the media. If there is a portrayal then it is not positive. They are portrayed as people without morals and sexually promiscuous.

20 Cremation is the accepted form of disposal of the body, since the body, along with its constituent parts is just clothing for the soul and is discarded at death.

21 Sikhs believe in reincarnation. This means that a person's soul may be reborn many times as a human or an animal. Sikhs believe

that there are 8,400,000 forms of life and that many souls have to travel through a number of these before they can reach *Waheguru*. When something dies the soul is reborn. It is only when one becomes a human that there is a chance of the cycle being broken because only humans know the difference between right and wrong.

Chapter 5

1 The *Khalsa* was created to preserve the Sikh way of life against Mughal threats. Guru Gobind Singh saw that if the way of life Sikhs believed in was to survive, then those who believed in it must be ready to fight to the death. The *Khalsa* was a way of forming a distinct Sikh identity, separate from Hinduism and Islam, while also making it more difficult for Sikhs to flee or deny their faith. For additional reasons for the formation of the *Khalsa*, see Hew McLeod, *Sikhism* (1997), 53–4, 111–16, and *Who is a Sikh* (1989b). McLeod suggests four distinct answers for the reasons behind the creation of the *Khalsa*, yet points out that they are only theories and that these debates remain open to debate.

2 The Singh Sabha was a reform movement begun in 1873 (McLeod 1989a, p. 145), in response to a religious community that was losing its members because Christian, Muslim and Hindu 'missionaries' were attempting to convert members of the Sikh community. The Hindu Arya Samaj, in particular, attempted to reintegrate into Hinduism what it saw as lapsed groups, which included the Sikhs (Singh and Tatla 2006; p. 17). The Singh Sabha sought to not only resist the proselytizing actions of these groups but also to gain recognition of Sikhs as a religious community in their own right, rather than just another Hindu sect; the slogan '*Ham Hindu Nai*' translates as 'we are not Hindus'. It also sought to eradicate what it saw as a Hindu influence within Sikhism. At this point in its history, the Sikh community had in many ways reverted to Hindu practices; caste distinctions were observed alongside notions of 'untouchability'. Outcastes were not allowed to enter many Gurdwaras and the *karah prasad* (sweet dough mixture given to visitors at a Gurdwara) was preserved from their 'contamination' (McLeod 1989b, p. 69).

3 The British pressed upon all their Sikh army recruits to comply with *Khalsa* dress, which served to give Sikhs a distinct identity and a degree of separateness from other recruits.

4 The outward symbols of Sikh faith are the most publically recognizable aspects of a *amritdhari* and *keshdhari* Sikh.

5 Some Sikhs would not put the *Gora* Sikhs into this hierarchy – they are not viewed to be true Sikhs because they have no Punjabi heritage.

6 One sheds one's surname, which is an indication of caste, and takes on a casteless surname of 'Singh', meaning lion for men, and 'Kaur', meaning princess for women. However, these names are often used even if you are not baptized. These names are a clear indication of a person's Sikh identity but not necessarily whether they are baptized or not.

7 *Kesh* is also, in the case of men, normally accompanied by the wearing of a turban or, if the hair is not particularly long (as in young boys) a top knot. The turban is considered of vital importance to men for a variety of reasons (hygiene for example), but mostly because of the importance placed on tying the *kesh* in a top knot and keeping it neat and tidy; the turban is the best practical method of achieving this (McLeod in Singh and Barrier 1999, p. 61). Women are not expected to wear the turban; but some particularly devout Sikh women have chosen to wear it (*Rehat Maryada*, Chapter 10, http://sgpc.net/rehat_maryada/section_four.html).

8 It is important to note that while they may observe the Five Ks, not all baptized Sikhs observe the rule of equality. Many believe and operate within the realm of caste. They justify their partial observance by pointing out that the Sikh Gurus did not necessarily adhere to their own teachings strictly; for example, the Gurus married within their own caste.

9 Guru Hargobind first introduced the idea of a saint-soldier, but it was not until the time of Guru Gobind Singh and the creation of the *Khalsa* that this concept reached its apex. All Sikhs who belong to the *Khalsa* should uphold the duties of a saint-soldier.

10 Takhar argues that the Sikh Dharama of the Western Hemisphere and the 3HO, both established by Yogi Bhajan, are at times two different groups and at other times one group. She argues that 3HO places an emphasis on *Kundalini yoga*, while the Sikh Dharma of the Western Hemisphere not only practices *Kundalini yoga*, but also practices and follows Sikh teachings.

11 There are no real figures about how many *Gora* Sikhs there are.

12 Sikhism is not a missionary religion. Sikhs believe that you should live within the religion that you are born. To convert to another religion or to try to convert someone means that you are questioning God's Will (*hukam*).

13 There are other legal cases in the United Kingdom which touch on
    Sikh identity: the 1976 Motor-cycle Crash-Helmets (Religious
    Exemption) Bill (http://hansard.millbanksystems.com/lords/1976/
    oct/04/motor-cycle-crash-helmets-religious); and Wearing Kirpan
    (sword) at the workplace and in society (Criminal Justice Act 1988
    and 1996). See also Takhar (2005) and Singh and Tatla (2006).
14 Mandla (Sewa Singh) and Another Appellant v. Dowell Lee and
    Others Respondents, http:// oxcheps.new.ox.ac.uk/new/casebook/
    cases/Cases%20Chapter%2011/Mandla%20v%20Dowell%20
    Lee.doc OR www.equalrightstrust.org/ertdocumentbank/Micro-
    soft%20Word%20-%20Mandla.pdf.
15 The UK Court Structure consists of
    (1) Magistrates Courts – deal with criminal, civil and family
        cases.
    (2) Crown Court – serious criminal cases are transferred from the
        magistrate's court.
    (3) County Court deals with serious civil cases.
    (4) Under the Umbrella of the Royal Courts of Justice we have the
        High Court and Court of Appeal. The High Court is made up
        of three divisions: Queen's Bench Division, Chancery Division
        and Family Division.
    (5) The Court of Appeal is made up of two divisions: Civil Divi-
        sion, which hears appeals referred from the High Court, and
        the Criminal Division which hears criminal cases from the
        Crown Courts.
    (6) The Supreme Court – final Court of Appeal in the United
        Kingdom, www.hmcourts-service.gov.uk/aboutus/structure/
        hol.htm, accessed 5 February 2009.
16 The notion of being a Sikh due to one's ethnic origin, rather than
    one's religion is further demonstrated by the current issue sur-
    rounding the inclusion of 'Sikh' in the census as an option for
    ethnic origin. Currently, the census only regards 'Sikh' as a reli-
    gious affiliation rather than an ethnic origin. The Commission for
    Racial Equality (CRE) has offered to place Sikh as a 'sub-category'
    under the Asian heading, but this has not satisfied the Sikhs. Sikhs
    do not want to be a sub-category, especially as many who put
    down Sikh for their religious category give Indian as their ethnic
    origin.
        The Sikh Federation (UK) actively campaigned to have 'Sikh'
    added as an ethnicity to the 2011 Census, but were unsuccesful. As

a result, Sikh organizations, through the media have been asking Sikhs to write the word Sikh in the 'Other' category under Ethnic Origin in the 2011 Census.

This is further evidence of the link in (at least some) British Sikhs' minds that they are an ethnicity. But what does it mean to be 'ethnically' Sikh? Could it be seen as synonymous with 'ethnically Punjabi'? If we consider the evidence then the answer must be a resounding 'no'. This is due to the fact that there are ethnically Punjabi peoples who are not Sikhs. Not only this, but different Sikhs are from different ethnic origins as well; jats are considered to be an Indo-Scythian people (or at least to have Scythian ancestry in part) (Nijjar 2008, pp. 44–5), whereas other Punjabis will be Indo-Aryan. Even without counting this, where do the 'Gora' Sikhs (Westerners who have converted to Sikhism) belong? Are they entitled to the same treatment under the law?

17 29 July 2008 verdict.

18 Audrey Gillian, *The Guardian*, 30 July 2008, ' "Proud to be Welsh and a Sikh". Schoolgirl wins court battle to wear religious bangle', http://www.guardian.co.uk/education/2008/jul/30/schools. religion.

19 The Human Rights Act 1998 incorporates the European Convention of Human Rights into UK Law, which includes Article 9 Freedom of Thought, Conscience and Religion:

  (1) Everyone has the right to freedom of thought, conscience and religion; this right includes freedom to change his religion or belief and freedom, either alone or in a community with others and in public or private, to manifest his religion or belief, in worship, teach, practice and observance.

  (2) Freedom to manifest one's religion or beliefs shall be subject only to such limitations as are prescribed by law and are necessary in a democratic society in the interests of public safety, for the protection of public order, health or morals, or for the protection of the rights and freedoms of others (cited in Edge 1998).

20 A Christian British Airways (BA) employee, Nadia Eweida, lost her claim against BA, her employer, for not allowing her to wear openly a Christian Cross on a chain over her uniform. British Airways had argued that there was a ban on all visible jewellery to maintain a uniform corporate image. Although the law states that employers should make allowances for items of clothing such as turbans or burkas, BA in this case were able to successfully

argue that the crucifix is not a compulsory item of Christian dress, just like the *kara* is not compulsory for a Sikh who is not baptized (www.guardian.co.uk/uk/2010/feb/12/christian-british-airways-workers-cross).

21 'Traditional' cannot be straightforwardly equated with stability and longevity (Brubaker in Ballard 2000). Also in such debates, past ancestral traditions and practices represent the 'good' and 'innocent', with Western culture being posed as 'bad', 'corrupt' and 'seductive' (Ballard 2000).

22 It is important to note that many baptized Sikhs also practice and follow cultural traditions such as caste endogamous marriages and dowry giving.

23 For example, caste identity is an example of a cultural phenomenon that is so ingrained within the Sikh psyche that it has become synonymous with religious identity. The Sikh religion in the twenty-first century is not free from castes (McLeod 2000). Instead, it has an exaggerated significance in the diaspora (Bradby 2007), which is evident through caste-based gurdwaras in the United Kingdom (Kalsi 1992), such as the Ramgharia Sikh Temple, Birmingham; Ramgarhia Sikh Gurdwara, Forest Gate, London; Guru Nanak Gurdwara Bhatra Singh Sabha, Preston; and Gurdwara Guru Nanak Bhatra Singh Sabha and Community Centre, Birmingham. Their presence demonstrates that Sikhs do identify themselves on the Basis of caste, and do go against one of the central tenets of Sikhism.

24 For example, in 2008 there was a fight for the control of Sri Guru Singh Sabha Gurdwara, London (March 2008), and abroad in January 1997 there was the struggle of Guru Nanak Gurdwara, Surrey, BC, Canada.

25 This does not apply to convert Sikhs who are defined Sikh through their religious practice.

Appendix

1 The word 'round' appears in all the verses at the beginning and the end, and it refers to the circumambulation of the Guru Granth Sahib by the bride and the groom.

Bibliography

Preface

Banerjee, Anil Chandra (1983), *The Sikh Gurus and the Sikh Religion*. Delhi: Munshiram Manoharlal.

Gatrad, A. R. et al. (eds) (2005), *Palliative Care for South Asians: Muslims, Hindus and Sikhs*. London: Quay Books.

McLeod, W. H. (1997), *Sikhism*. London: Penguin.

Singh, Gurharpal and Tatla, D. S. (2006), *Sikhs in Britain: The Making of a Community*. London: Zed Books.

Singh, Khushwant (1977), A History of the Sikhs, Vols 1 and 2. New Delhi: Oxford University Press.

Chapter 1

Banerjee, Anil Chandra (1983), *The Sikh Gurus and the Sikh Religion*. Delhi: Munshiram Manoharlal.

Bhachu, Parminder (1985), *Twice Migrants: East African Sikh Settlers in Britain*. London: Tavistock.

Buck, P. S. (1987), From the Forward to the, *Translation of Guru Granth Sahib* by Gopal Singh, pXIX, 1, 7th edn., New Delhi: Allied.

Cole, W. O., and Sambhi, P. S. (1978), *The Sikhs: Their Religious Beliefs and Practices*. London: Routledge & Keegan Paul.

Field, Dorothy (1914), *The Religion of the Sikhs*. London: John Murray.

Gatrad, A. R., Jhutti-Johal, J., Gill, P., and Sheikh, A. (2005), 'Sikh birth customs'. *Archives of Diseases in Childhood*, 90, 560–3.

McLeod, W. H. (1997), *Sikhism*. London: Penguin.

Singh, Daljeet (1994), *Sikhism: A Comparative Study of Its Theology and Mysticism* (2nd edn). Amritsar: Singh Brothers.

Singh, Gopal (1978), *Sri Guru Granth Sahib*. English Version. 4 Vols. Chandigarh, India: World Sikh University Press.
Singh, Jodh and Singh, Dharam (1999), *Sri Dasam Granth Sahib: Text and Translation*. 2 Vols. Patiala, India: Heritage.
Singh, Khushwant (1977), *A History of the Sikhs*, Vol. 1. New Delhi: Oxford University Press.
Singh, Patwant (1999), *The Sikhs*. London: John Murray, 28.

Chapter 2

The American Academy for the Advancement of Science, and the National Institutes of Health (2001), cited in Thomas B. Okarma, 'Human embryonic stem cells: a primer on the technology and its medical applications', in S. Holland, H. Lebacqz, and Laurie Zoloth (eds), *The Human Embryonic Stem Cell Debate*. Cambridge, MA: MIT Press.
Banerjee, Anil Chandra (1983), *The Sikh Gurus and the Sikh Religion*. Delhi: Munshiram Manoharlal.
Bapteste, E., and Walsh, D. A. (2005), 'Does the "Ring of Life" ring true?', *Trends in Microbiology*, 13, 6, 256–61.
Corrigan, O., Liddell, K., McMillan, J., Stewart, A., and Wallace, S. (2006), *Ethical, Legal and Social Issues in Stem Cell Research and Therapy*. A briefing paper from Cambridge Genetics Knowledge Park.
Darwin, C. (1985), *The Origin of Species by Means of Natural Selection: Or The Preservation of Favoured Races in the Struggle for Life*. New York: Penguin Classics.
Dawkins, R. (1997), *River Out of Eden*. London: Harper Collins.
Futuyma, Douglas J. (2005), *Evolution*. Sunderland, MA: Sinauer Associates, Inc.
Hawkins, Stephen (1995), *A Brief History of Time: From the Big Bang to Black Holes*. New York: Bantam Books.
McLeod, W. H. (1968), *Guru Nanak and the Sikh Religion*. Oxford: Clarendon Press.
— (1975), *The Evolution of the Sikh Community*. New Delhi: Oxford University Press.
— (1989), *The Sikhs. History, Religion and Society*. New York: Columbia University Press.
— (1992), *Who is a Sikh?* Oxford: Clarendon Press.
— (1997), *Sikhism*. London: Penguin.
Singh, Gopal (1978), *Sri Guru Granth Sahib*. English Version. 4 Vols. Chandigarh, India: World Sikh University Press.

Singh, Harbans (1969), *Guru Nanak and the Origins of the Sikh Faith*. Bombay: Asia Publishing House.

Singh, Jodh (1999), *Sikh Religion and Human Civilization*. Patiala: Punjabi University Publication Department.

— (2000), *Outlines of Sikh Philosophy*. Patiala: Punjabi University Publication Department.

Singh, Simon (2004), *Big Bang*. London: Harper Collins.

Singh, Teja (1968), *The Sikh Religion: An Outline of Its Doctrines*. Amritsar: Shiromani Gurdwara Prabandhak Committee.

United Nations Educational, Scientific and Cultural Organization (2005), *Ethical Issues*. France: UNESCO.

Chapter 3

Banerjee, Anil Chandra (1983), *The Sikh Gurus and the Sikh Religion*. Delhi: Munshiram Manoharlal.

Bhachu, Parminder (1985), *Twice Migrants: East African Sikh Settlers in Britain*. London and New York: Tavistock.

— (1986), 'Work, marriage and dowry among East African Sikh women in the United Kingdom', in R. J. Simon and C. B. Brettell (eds), *International Migration: The Female Experience*. Totowa, NJ: Rowman and Allanheld.

Census of India (2001), "Provisional Population Totals: India." www. censusindia.net/results/prov_pop_main.html (accessed 10 October 2009).

Christ, Carol (1980), *Diving Deep and Surfacing: Women Writers on Spiritual Quest*. Boston: Beacon Press.

— (1985), 'Symbols of goddess and god in feminist theology', in Carl Olson (ed.), *Book of the Goddess*. New York: Crossroad.

Cole, W. O., and Sambhi, P. S. (1985), *The Sikhs: Their Beliefs and Practices*. London: Routledge and Kegan Paul (Reprint with corrections of the original book dated 1978).

Daly, Mary (1973), *Beyond God the Father: Toward a Philosophy of Women's Liberation*. Boston: Beacon Press.

Doniger, W. and Brian Smith (1991) (trans.), *The Law of Manu*. New York: Penguin Classics.

Dubuc, S., and Coleman, D. (2007), 'An increase in the sex ratio of births to India-born mothers in England and Wales: Evidence for sex-selective abortion', *Population and Development Review*, 33, 383–400.

Dusenbery, V. A. (1998), 'Punjabi Sikhs and Gora Sikhs: conflicting assertions of Sikh identity in North America', in O'Connell, et al.

(eds), *Sikh History and Religion in the Twentieth Century*. New Delhi: Manohar.

Indian Government 57 of 1994 (1994), india.gov.in/allimpfrms/allacts/1623.pdf (accessed 26 April 2009).

Jakobsh, Doris R. (2003), *Relocating Gender in Sikh History: Transformation, Meaning and Identity*. India: Oxford University Press.

Jha, P., Kumar, R., Vasa, P., Dhingra, N., Thiruchelvam, D., and Moineddin, R. (2006), 'Low male-to-female sex ratio of children born in India: national survey of 1.1 million households'. *The Lancet*, 367, 9506, 211–8.

Jhutti, J. (1998), 'Dowry among Sikhs in Britain', in Werner Menski (ed.), *South Asians and the Dowry Problem*. Stoke on Trent: Trentham Books.

— (2010), 'The role of women in their religious institutions: a contemporary account', in Doris Jakobsch (ed.), *Sikhism and Women: History, Texts and Experience*. India: Oxford University Press.

Kaur, Upinderjit (1990), *Sikh Religion and Economic Development*. New Delhi: National Book Organisation.

Khalsa, S. K. (1995), *The History of the Sikh Sharma of the Western Hemisphere*. Espanola, New Mexico: Sikh Dharma Publications.

Lahori, Lajwanti. (1995). *The Concept of Man in Sikhism*. New Delhi: Munshiram Manoharlal.

McCormack, Manjeet Kaur (1985), *The Sikh Marriage Ceremony*. Edgware: Sikh Cultural Society of Great Britain.

McLeod, W. H. (1968), *Guru Nanak and the Sikh Religion*. Oxford: Clarendon Press.

— (1989a), *The Sikhs: History, Religion and Society*, New York/Chichester: Columbia University Press.

— (1997), *Sikhism*. London: Penguin.

Menski, Werner (1998), *South Asians and the Dowry Problem*. Stoke on Trent: Trentham Books.

Olivelle, Patrick, (2004). *The Law Code of Manu* (a new translation). Oxford: Oxford University Press.

Pinkham, Mildreth (1967), *Woman in the Sacred Scriptures of Hinduism*. New York: AMS.

Pruthi, R., and Sharma, R. B. (1995), *Sikhism and Women*. New Delhi: Anmol Publications.

Puwar, N., and Raghuram, P. (2003), *South Asian Women in the Diaspora*. Oxford: Berg Publishers.

Reuther, Rosemary Radford (1975), *New Woman New Earth: Sexist Ideologies and Human Liberation*. New York: Seabury Press.

— (1983), *Sexism and God-Talk: Toward a Feminist Theology*. Boston: Beacon Press.

Sen, A. K. (1992), 'Missing women'. *British Medical Journal*, 304, 586–7.

— (2003), 'Missing women – revisited : reduction in female mortality has been counterbalanced by sex selective abortions'. *British Medical Journal*, 327 (6 December), 1297–8.

Sen, Mala (2002), *Death by Fire: Sati, Dowry Death and Female Infanticide in Modern India*. New Brunswick, NJ: Rutgers University Press.

Shiromani Gurdwara Prabandhak Committee (1950), *The Rehat Maryada*. Amritsar, Punjab, India.

Singh, Gopal (1978), *Sri Guru Granth Sahib*, English Version, 4 Vols. Chandigarh, India: World Sikh University Press.

Singh, Gurharpal, and Tatla, D. S. (2006), *Sikhs in Britain: The Making of a Community*. London: Zed Books.

Singh, Gurnam (2006), 'Sikhism's emancipatory discourses: some critical perspectives'. *Sikh Formations*, 2 (2), 135–51.

Singh, Khuswant (1991), *History of the Sikhs*, Vol. 2. Oxford: Oxford University Press.

Singh, Nikky Guninder Kaur (1993), *The Feminine Principle in the Sikh Vision of the Transcendent*. Cambridge: Cambridge University Press.

— (2005a), 'Re-membering the body of the transcendent one'. *Sikh Formations*, 1 (2), 201–16.

— (2005b), *The Birth of the Khalsa: A Feminist Re-Memory of Sikh Identity*. Albany, NY: State University of New York Press.

— (2008), 'Female feticide in the Punjab and fetus imagery in Sikhism', in Vanessa R. Sasson and Jane Marie Law (eds), *Imagining the Fetus: the Unborn in Myth, religion and Culture*. New York: Oxford University Press.

Takhar, Opinderjit Kaur (2005), *Sikh Identity: An exploration of Groups Among Sikhs*. London: Ashgate.

Talib, G. S. (1987), *Sri Guru Granth Sahib*, English Translation. Patiala, India: Punjabi University Press.

Taneja, Taneja (2009), 'MP demands law against dowries'. BBC Asian Network. http://news.bbc.co.uk/1/hi/uk/8093948.stm (accessed 30 October 2009).

Chapter 4

Ballard, R. (1972), 'Family organisation among the Sikhs in Britain'. *New Community,* 2 (1), 12–24.

— (1982), 'South Asian Families', in R. N. Rapport (ed.), *Families in Britain.* London: Routledge.

Banerjee, Anil Chandra (1983), *The Sikh Gurus and the Sikh Religion.* Delhi: Munshiram Manoharlal.

Census of India (2001), 'Provisional Population Totals: India'. www.censusindia.net/results/prov_pop_main.html (accessed 10 October 2009).

Gatrad, A. R., Jhutti-Johal, J., Gill, P. S., and Sheikh, A. (2005), Sikh Birth Customs. *Archives of Diseases in Childhood* 90: 560–3.

Handyside, Alan, H., and Jay D. A. Delhanty (1997), 'Preimplantation genetic diagnosis: strategies and surprises'. *Trends in Genetics,* 13 (7), 270–75.

House of Commons Science and Technology Select Committee (2007), Scientific Developments Relating to the Abortion Act 1967.

Jha, P., Kumar, R., Vasa, P., Dhingra, N., Thiruchelvam, D., and Moineddin, R. (2006), 'Low male-to-female sex ratio of children born in India: national survey of 1.1 million households'. *The Lancet,* 367 (9506), 211–18.

Jhutti-Johal, Jagbir (1998), 'A study of changes in marriage practices among the Sikhs of Britain'. DPhil Thesis. Oxford: Oxford University.

— (2007), 'What Makes a Good City?': A Sikh Perspective in *'What Makes a Good City?' Faith Perspectives,* Birmingham: University of Birmingham.

McLeod, W. H. (1968), *Guru Nanak and the Sikh Religion.* Oxford: Clarendon Press.

— (1997), *Sikhism.* London: Penguin.

The Pre-Natal Diagnostic Techniques (Regulation and Prevention of Misuse) Act No. 57 of 1994 [20th September, 1994]: india.gov.in/allimpfrms/allacts/1623.pdf (accessed 26 April 2009).

Robertson, J. A. (2003), 'Extending preimplantation genetic diagnosis: ethical issues in new uses of preimplantation genetic diagnosis'. *Human Reproduction,* 18 (3), 465–71.

Russell, Betrand (1996), *Marriage and Morals.* London: Routledge.

Sen, A. K. (1992), 'Missing women', *British Medical Journal,* 304, 586–7.

— (2003), 'Missing somen – revisited: reduction in female mortality has been counterbalanced by sex selective abortions'. *British Medical Journal* 27 (6 December), 1297–8.

Sen, Mala (2002), *Death by Fire: Sati, Dowry Death and Female Infanticide in Modern India*. New Brunswick, NJ: Rutgers University Press.

Sermon, K. A. Van Steirtegham, and Liebaers, I. (2004), 'Preimplantation genetic diagnosis'. *The Lancet*, 363 (9421), 1633–41.

Shiromani Gurdwara Prabandhak Committee (1950), *The Rehat Maryada*. Amritsar, Punjab, India.

Singh, Avtar (1996), *Ethics of the Sikhs*. Patiala: Punjabi University Publication Department.

Singh, Gopal (1978), *Sri Guru Granth Sahib*, English Version, 4 Vols. Chandigarh, India: World Sikh University Press.

Singh, Nikky Guninder Kaur (2005b), *The Birth of The Khalsa: A Feminist Re-Memory of Sikh Identity*. Albany, NY: State University of New York Press.

Singh, Nirpinder (1990), *The Sikh Moral Tradition*. New Delhi: Manohar.

Soch, H. S., and Madanjit Kaur (1998), *Guru Nanak: Ideals and Institutions*. Amritsar: Guru Nank Dev University.

Talib, G. S. (1987), *Sri Guru Granth Sahib*, English Translation. Patiala, India: Punjabi University Press.

Vardy, Peter, and Paul Grosch (1999), *The Puzzle of Ethics*. London: Harper Collins.

Chapter 5

Agniholm, Rama Kant (1983), *Crisis of Identity: Sikhs in England*. New Delhi: Bahri.

All England Law Report (1982), Vol. 3. London: Butterworth and Co.

— (1983), Vol. 1, (House of Lords). London: Butterworth and Co.

Ballard, R. (ed.) (1994), *Desh Pardesh: The South Asian Presence in Britain*. London: Hurst & Co.

Baumann, Gerd (1996), *Contesting Culture: Discourses of Identity in Multi-Ethnic London*. Cambridge: Cambridge University Press.

Bradby, Hannah (2007), 'Watch out for the aunties! Young British Asians' accounts of identity and substance use'. *Sociology of Health and Illness*, 29 (5), 656–72.

Cole, W. O., and Sambhi, P. S. (1985), *The Sikhs: Their Beliefs and Practices*. London: Routledge and Kegan Paul (Reprint with corrections of the original book dated 1978).

— (1990), *A Popular Dictionary of Sikhism*. London: Curzon.

— (1993), *Sikhism and Christianity; A Comparative Study*. Houndmills, Basingstoke: Macmillan Press.

Deol, Jeevan. (2001), 'The Eighteenth Century Khalsa Identity: Discourse, Praxis and Narrative'. in C. Shackle, G. Singh and A. P. Mandair (eds) *Sikh Religion, Culture and Ethnicity*. Surrey: Curzon Press.

Dusenbery, V. A. (1988), 'Punjabi Sikhs and Gora Sikhs: Conflicting Assertion of Sikh Identity in North America'. in Joseph T, O'Connell, et al., (eds) *Sikh History and Religion in the Twentieth Century*. Toronto Centre for South Asian Studies: University of Toronto.

— (1997), 'The poetics and politics of recognition: diasporan Sikhs in pluralist polities'. *American Ethnologist*, 24 (4), 738–62.

Edge, Peter W. (1998), 'The European court of human rights and religious rights'. *Comparative Law Quarterly*, 47, 680–7.

Gillan, Audrey (2008), 'Proud to be Welsh and a Sikh: schoolgirl wins court battle to wear religious bangle'. *The Guardian Online* www.guardian.co.uk/education/2008/jul/30/schools.religion (accessed 8 January 2010).

Grewal, J. S. (2008), *The Sikhs of the Punjab* (Revised Edition). Cambridge: Cambridge University Press.

Gupta, Dipankar (1996), *The Context of Ethnicity: Sikh Identity in a Comparative Perspective*. Delhi: Oxford University Press.

Her Majesty's Court Service: Court Structure www.hmcourts-service. gov.uk/aboutus/structure/hol.htm (accessed 5 February 2009).

Jakobsh, Doris (2008), '3HO/Sikh Dharma of the Western hemisphere: the "forgotten" new religious movement?' *Religious Compass*, 2 (3), 385–408.

Kalsi, S. S. (1992), *The Evolution of the Sikh Community in Britain: Religious and Social Change Among the Sikhs of Leeds and Bradford*. Leeds: University of Leeds.

Kaur, Birendra (2001), *On Sikh Identity*. Amritsar: Singh Brothers.

Kaur, Madanjit (ed.) (2000), *Guru Gobind Singh and the Creation of the Khalsa*. Amritsar: Guru Nanak Dev University.

Madan, T. N. (1998), 'Coping with ethnicity in South Asia: Bangladesh, Punjab and Kashmir compared'. *Ethnic and Racial Studies*, 25 (5), 969–89.

Mann, G. S. (2000), Sikhism in the United States of America, in Harold G.Coward, John R Hinnells and Raymond Brady Willians (eds). *The South Asian Religious Diaspora in Britain, Canada and the United States*. Albany, NY: State University of New York, 259–77.

McLeod, W. H. (1968), *Guru Nanak and the Sikh Religion*. Oxford: Clarendon Press.

— (1989a), *The Sikhs: History, Religion and Society*, New York/ Chichester: Columbia University Press.

— (1989b), *Who Is a Sikh? The Problem of Sikh Identity*. Oxford: Clarendon Press.

— (1997), *Sikhism*. London: Penguin.

— (1999), 'Discord in the Sikh Panth'. *Journal of the American Oriental Society*, 119 (3), 381–9.

— (2000), *Exploring Sikhism – Aspects of Sikh Identity, Culture and Thought*. Oxford: Oxford University Press.

Nesbitt, E. (2000), *The Religious Lives of Sikh Children: a Coventry-Based Study*. Leeds: University of Leeds.

Nijjar, B. S. (2008), *Origins and History of Jats and Other Allied Nomadic Tribes of India*. New Delhi: Atlantic Publishers and Distributors.

Oberoi, Harjot (1992), 'Popular saints, goddesses, and village sacred sites: rereading Sikh experience in the nineteenth century'. *History of Religions*, 31 (4), 363–84.

Purewal, S. (2000), *Sikh Ethnonationalism and the Political Economy of the Punjab*. Oxford: Oxford University Press.

Rait, S. K. (2005), *Sikh Women in England: their Religious and Cultural Beliefs and Social Practices*. Stoke on Trent/Sterling: Trentham Books.

Shiromani Gurdwara Prabandhak Committee (1994), *Sikh Rehat Maryada*, http://sgpc.net/sikhism/sikh-dharma-manual.html (accessed 10 July 2009).

Sidhu, M. S. (1993), *Sikhs in Thailand*. Asian Monographs No. 049. Bangkok, Thailand: Institute of Asian Studies, Chulalongkorn University.

Singh, Gurharpal, and Tatla, D. S. (2006), *Sikhs in Britain: The Making of a Community*. London: Zed Books Ltd.

Singh, Pashuara, and Barrier, N. G. (eds) (1998), *The Transmission of Sikh Heritage in the Diaspora*. New Delhi: Manohar.

— (1999), *Sikh Identity: Continuity and Change*. New Delhi: Manohar.

Singh, Patwant (1999), *The Sikhs*. London: John Murray.

Singh, Ramindar (1992), *Immigrants to Citizens: The Sikh Community in Bradford*. Bradford: Race Relations Research Unit.

Singh, Sangat (1995), *The Sikhs in History*. New York: Sangat Singh.

Sunaina, Maira. (1999), 'Identity Dub: The Paradoxes of an Indian Youth Subculture' (New York Mix). *Cultural Anthropology*, 14 (1), 29–60.

Takhar, Opinderjit Kaur (2005), *Sikh Identity: An Exploration of Groups among Sikhs*. Hants: Ashgate.

Tatla, D. S. (2001), 'Imagining Punjab – narratives of nationhood and homeland among the Sikh diaspora', in C. Shackle, et al. (eds), *Sikh Religion, Culture and Ethnicity*. London: Curzon Press.

Tatla, D. S. (2005), 'Sikh Diaspora', in Melvin Ember, Carol R. Ember, and Ian Skoggard (eds), *Encyclopedia of Diasporas*. New York: Springer.

Chapter 6

Ballard, R. (ed.) (1994), *Desh Pardesh. The South Asian Presence in Britain*. London: Hurst & Co.

— (1994a), 'The emergence of Desh Pardesh', in *Desh Pardesh: The South Asian Presence in Britain*. London: Hurst & Co.

— (1994b), 'Differentiation and disjunction', in *Desh Pardesh. The South Asian Presence in Britain*. London: Hurst & Co.

Singh, Gurharpal, and Tatla, D. S. (2006), *Sikhs in Britain: The Making of a Community*. London: Zed Books.

Appendix

Singh, Narain (1978), *Spirit Marriage*. Patiala: Guru Nanak Dev Mission.

Wylam, P. M (n.d.), *The Sikh Marriage Ceremony*. Publication no. 15. Kent: The Sikh Missionary Society.

Index